STAFF DEVELOPMENT
FOR
THE PRACTITIONER

STAFF DEVELOPMENT FOR THE PRACTITIONER

Planning • Procedures • Practices • Assessment

By

MARGARET E. FITCH, ED.D.

*Assistant Superintendent
Staff Development Services
Omaha Public Schools
Omaha, Nebraska*

and

O. W. KOPP, ED.D.

*University of Nebraska, Lincoln
Teachers College
Center for Curriculum and Instruction
Lincoln, Nebraska*

CHARLES C THOMAS • PUBLISHER
Springfield • Illinois • U.S.A.

Published and Distributed Throughout the World by

CHARLES C THOMAS • PUBLISHER
2600 South First Street
Springfield, Illinois 62794-9265

© *1990 by* CHARLES C THOMAS • PUBLISHER

ISBN 0-398-05661-7

Library of Congress Catalog Card Number: 89-48082

Printed in the United States of America
SC-R-3

Library of Congress Cataloging-in-Publication Data

Fitch, Margaret E.
    Staff development for the practitioner : planning, procedures,
practices, assessment / by Margaret E. Fitch and O. W. Kopp.
        p.   cm.
    Includes bibliographical references.
    ISBN 0-398-05661-7
    1. Teachers—In-service training.   2. School employees—In-service
training.   3. School personnel management.   I. Kopp, O. W. (Oswald
W.), 1918-   . II. Title.
LB1731.F52   1990
371.1'46—dc20   89-48082
                                                                                CIP

To Marie Kopp, Jan and Betsy Rogers; Lloyd, Sherry,
Jennifer, Suzy, and Katy Fitch—
—Our constant inspiration!

FOREWORD

Staff development encompasses everyone who is employed within a school system or any educational endeavor. Personnel need training and assistance to become the best they can be. This includes teachers, supervisors, administrators, secretaries, support staff, maintenance, and transportation personnel—everyone on the payroll. Societal changes are on-going and staff development is one of the proven means to provide professionals with planned programs and training to improve performance. Improved productivity is acquired as the result of staff empowerment to achieve change.

It is hoped that this publication will provide direction for problem identification, program planning, wise utilization of human and material resources, delivering the program content, and assessing results. The emphasis is on the practical and the "How To," by helping the practioner with the procedural process.

School people are extremely busy individuals. Their major function is to educate the student. Yet, too often much valuable time is dissipated by perceived unnecessary meetings and meaningless planning sessions. However, by carefully structuring the organization and providing ownership in decision making, professional learning can be the avenue to success for all.

To this end the writers have directed their efforts.

CONTENTS

STAFF DEVELOPMENT
FOR
THE PRACTITIONER

CHAPTER 1

SOCIETAL DEMANDS AND STAFF DEVELOPMENT

The school serves as a mirror reflecting the changing and escalating demands of society. The classroom teachers' concerns of how to deal with such "noncurricular" issues as AIDS, drugs, alcohol, and juvenile crime represents a few of the frustrations faced by professionals. Additional concern must be shown for educators as they walk a curricular tightrope for every lesson prepared and taught, so as not to offend some constituency in the community. Teachers and schools at times appear to be targets of unreasonable expectations. Staff need support and help in coping with the ever-increasing demands of the community. The challenge is to provide ways and means to help professionals grow on the job, as well as in gaining assistance in order to deal with the evolving curriculum. A staff development program, carefully designed to meet the pressing needs of the current era, represents the best approach to meeting the escalating challenges of modern society placed upon our schools.

The purpose is not to be protective of the public school. Rather, the purpose is to highlight the complexity of societal issues. Education is the top "business" in every state. It has its problems, its supporters, and critics. The challenge is for all facets of society to try to resolve society's common problems.

Since the publication of *A Nation At Risk: The Imperative for Educational Reform,* many reports have followed which enunciate policies and procedures for improving the schools of this nation. The extended school year, teacher improvement, and greater demands in core subjects have been but few of the responses to strengthen the schools' ability to cope with escalating demands. The challenge now lies with long-range planning and the updating of teacher skills through staff development training programs. Such programs can be the means to provide professional growth in order that staff may keep up with continuing change and challenges.

THE SCHOOL'S RESPONSIBILITY

What, exactly, is the responsibility of the school? When the chips are down, the bottom line demands results in "the basics," a term with many definitions. Usually, the focus is upon communication skills, math, and science. So, why don't schools remain within this area of responsibility? "The basics," operationally, are a very fluid commodity. The parent whose child is remotely musical or athletically inclined soon makes it known that "the basics" include music and athletics.

Perhaps it is time for this nation to seriously ask, what indeed are the priorities of this institution called "school?" Also, perhaps the time has come to ask, what is the home's responsibility relative to the child's readiness to come to school for a day's learning? The writers recall the sage statement of a respected, experienced elementary school principal: "Send us a happy, healthy child and we will educate him." Little by little, crisis by crisis, the school has become a surrogate parent, and not always with legal support. What can be done to see that the home holds up its end of the bargain in educating children? The need for genuine assistance for professional staff is obvious. Many approaches for rendering assistance have been tried with varied success. Shortcomings in attempts to assist professionals have been: (1) lack of identification of the genuine problems bothersome to teachers, (2) lack of planning in presenting inservice materials, (3) lack of involvement of key personnel, and (4) lack of follow-up in application of inservice material. Staff development can deliver realistic assistance. Societal demands are *real.* Ways and means to assist teachers in coping with these challenges can be found in a well-structured staff development program.

WHAT IS STAFF DEVELOPMENT?

Improved instruction is the goal of staff development. Effective staff development must constantly focus upon the goal of improved classroom instruction. Elements of quality staff development include the following:

1. building of common knowledge and concepts—delivering knowledge and concepts in a consistent manner. Each time staff development training is delivered, it should convey the same message.
2. shared vision—developing a shared vision among participants.

Staff development must include clear objectives. Those objectives must link what is to be learned in actual classroom practice.

3. change in values and beliefs—identifying desired changes in values and beliefs. For example, all children can learn. The staff development must hold the promise of meeting a need and showing a better method of instruction. Values and beliefs can be changed only when needs are met and change is shown to be useful.
4. supporting and translating new values and beliefs into specific behaviors—participants must be given the opportunity to see behavioral changes described in writing, modeled, and remodeled, and must be able to practice the designed behaviors. The desired behaviors that have evolved during staff development must be observed, redirected, and evaluated. This holds true for teachers and administrators.
5. systematic management of the resulting changes—using management to assure desired outcomes. In schools, the administration must find ways to manage new expected behaviors. These ways include involving staff in follow-up sessions, observations, evaluation, collaboration, and renewal activities.

Effective staff development will move professional staff from *what is,* to *what should be.* The key term is *change,* not change for the sake of change, but rather change for improved education.

THE "INTERNALIZATION" FACTOR

A fundamental tenet for involving teachers in any staff development process is "internalization." Unless a teacher fully understands and accepts a new program as something that will strengthen the quality of instruction, there is no reason to adopt a new approach. This represents a basic reason why curriculum development at the local school level has been encouraged. Admittedly, results have been far from perfect and products developed often are ragged at the edges, but in this way curriculum development becomes the product of teachers' effort. Because it is *their* product, chances for its implementation are greater.

Ralph Tyler feels that "where the children are, is the important locus of curriculum development" (*Phi Delta Kappan,* 1981). Having worked with teachers and principals for three decades, the writers believe strongly that the internalization factor, the feeling that "this is *my* program," is paramount to successful implementation within the classroom. If the five guidelines are followed—staff development leadership and teachers are operating from the same knowledge base, there is agreement upon a set of common objectives, all desire change if it will be useful and modify behaviors—then the "internalization" process is underway. The proposed plan is progressing toward total implementation.

HISTORICAL PERSPECTIVES

Sputnik was launched by the Russians on October 4, 1957. The resulting impact upon American education was most provocative. Dollars, programs, and advice were showered upon public schools. The Russians had preceded the scientific community of the United States into space but, interestingly enough, the public school received the brunt of pressure for change. This became an opportune time for reflection and updating programs, especially in the fields of math and science. As a result, at the beginning of the 1960s public school curriculum placed heavy emphasis upon the sciences. For example, in Jerome S. Bruner's *The Process of Education* (1960), outcomes of a ten-day conference of thirty-five scientists, scholars, and educators are reported in terms of how science education in our primary and secondary schools could be improved. In the introduction, Bruner writes that there has been unprecedented participation in curriculum development by university scholars and scientists, persons distinguished for their work at the frontiers of their respective disciplines. The impact of this conference upon curriculum was significant, but not lasting.

B. F. Skinner's publication, *The Technology of Teaching* (1968), extolled the virtues of the teaching machine. Skinner states, "we have every reason to expect, therefore, that the most effective control of human learning will require instrumental aid." It is interesting to observe how the flow of societal events have an impact upon what is taught in public schools. Educators do not determine curriculum. Rather, schools serve as a mirror, reflecting and implementing the desires of a given community. For example, the introduction of the computer, another "instrumental aid," into virtually every classroom in the country is evidence of community wishes being fulfilled. Interestingly enough, in "Newsnotes" (*Phi Delta Kappan*, 1985), a report prepared by the National Commission for Employment Policy (NCEP) states that only 5 percent of all jobs require expertise in computers, and those jobs will account for no more than one percent of the work force by 1995. It is further stated that most other workers who use computers "can learn the necessary skills by brief training, from a few hours to a few weeks, followed by a period of learning in the course of work." Yet, pressure to incorporate the computer into instructional programs at every age level exists. Thus the computer, within a decade, has become part of the Warp and Woof of American society and the school curricula.

It has been stated previously that staff development is the best approach for assisting teachers in keeping pace with the rapidly evolving curriculum. For example, a decade ago no one was considering gang membership avoidance as part of the instructional program. Yet today's teachers need to understand more about the nature of this problem. The need for a mechanism to keep abreast of change is obvious. Staff development procedures to cope with the evolving social scene have not always been successful, yet potential for success is present if proper procedures are followed.

Two research reports by Gerald W. Bracey in "Research" (*Kappan,* September, 1988) state that the history of staff development has not always been illustrious. The findings of Thomas Guskey of the University of Kentucky reported that virtually every major work relating to staff development in the last 30 years emphasized shortcomings in effectiveness. Bracey also reports that Mark Symlie, of the University of Illinois at Chicago, indicates that most evaluations of staff development activities collect just a few statements concerning teachers' satisfaction with such activities. Few evaluations look at changes in teaching in a systematic way. Those which have done so have usually looked at only a limited set of variables.

Shortcomings in the staff development process emphasize the need for knowledgeable leadership in the planning, implementation, and on-going assessment of a successful program. Staff development leadership must know the research and application for the purpose of identifying genuine staff problems. Leaders must also know how to bring about meaningful change in selected areas. Change is inevitable. The professionals' challenge is to make sure that time and effort devoted to such activity represents improvement.

The staff development concept combines some of the best ingredients for assisting teachers. The inservice program is designed at the local level. It involves the staff; it identifies trained expertise to assist and can personalize a "packaged program" by implementing meaningful inservice activities. Staff development can represent the apex in the state of the art of helping teachers in this complex society. Thus, the content following in this publication is devoted to the "How To" of implementing a complete, meaningful, operational staff development program.

THE 21ST CENTURY AND STAFF DEVELOPMENT

The end of the nineteen eighties, no doubt, will go down in history as an era when the national administration got "tough" with educators and education. This approach, even though it produced considerable legislation, higher qualifications for teachers and numerous reforms at the local level, has not achieved basic restructuring on the home front. Many of these changes have been engineered by power structures outside the educational community. The feeling conveyed was that professional educators were often too defensive and unwilling to make required massive changes in the so-called education establishment. This resulted in the overt push to "get the job done" without the full cooperation of practitioners.

Calls for change during this era appeared to head in two diverse directions. The former Secretary of Education appeared to hammer away at the "more" approach to improvement—more homework, more hours in the school day, more days in the school year and certainly, more rigor in the curriculum. On the other hand, the futurists were pressing for collegial learning, teacher empowerment, creative independent thinking, understanding values, inquiry, problem solving, curriculum depth instead of coverage, use of technology, and global interdependence. In terms of needs both approaches are correct. Our children need both if they are to be ready to cope within an ever more complex society.

All in all, the lesson to be learned from the eighties is the fundamental principle that basic restructuring cannot be imposed from the top down. Internalization needed by those who implement new programs and practices will not occur if restructuring is imposed from the outside. A professional must truly feel this material to be imparted to children is vital and important, and have a voice in the formulation of its content. Empowerment of teachers in decision making is a vital link in guaranteeing programmatic success.

The underlying premise from studies such as the Mastery in Learning

Project of the National Education Association (McClure, 1988) is that change must come from within the school system. Laws from legislatures, directives from state boards of education, and pronouncements from the federal government may do more harm than good. This type of activity tends to impede rather than promote action at the local level.

We as a nation have listened to the policy makers outside of education without achieving excellence for our children. It may be time for a new format—a format represented by educators, a format for educators—hopefully supported by community, state, and nation. In an educator-based approach, adversarial positions between school and community must be resolved if meaningful change is to become reality. Change and improvement result from a cooperative base involving the vast majority of publics within a school system. For example, business interests in a community must become part of school change. A greater percentage of business involvements appear to be of the fringe variety. Lectures by business executives, money for scholarships, school visitations to the "plant" and, yes, even the "adopting" of a school represent good public relations, but not necessarily the resolution of fundamental problems of the educational community. Business and industry involvement represents a starting point, not an accomplished fact in program development. School leadership must initiate invitations to business representatives and other community representatives, and together resolve training and curricular issues. In this setting, it is possible that genuine restructuring can transpire.

The downfall of bringing about change does not, contrary to some common beliefs, primarily lie in the lack of ideas, but rather in the knowledge of how to transform an innovative idea into a viable operational plan. This plan, to be operational, must be placed into a setting where it is accepted and carried out by the professionals responsible for the full implementation of the innovation.

The vehicle of translating ideas into action rests with a carefully structured staff development program. Such a program involves knowledgeable people from various walks of life, sound staff development leadership from the professional educators, and a commitment from all to meet the challenge and restructure the existing format of education to meet the needs of the 21st century.

REFERENCES

Bruner, Jerome S. (1960). *The Process of Education.* New York, Vantage Books, p. 1.

Cox, P. L. (1983). "Complementary Roles in Successful Change." *Educational Leadership,* Vol. 41, No. 3, pp. 10–13.

Fitzgerald, Francis. (1979). *America Revised.* Little Brown & Company.

Loucks, S. and Lieberman, A. (1983). "Curriculum Implementation." *Fundamental Curriculum Decisions.* Alexandria, Virginia, Association for Supervision and Curriculum Development, p. 127.

Guskey, T. R. (1985). Staff Development and Teacher Change. *Educational Leadership,* Vol. 42, No. 7, pp. 57–60.

Edelfett, R. A. (1986). Staff Development in the Next 10 Years. *The Journal of Staff Development,* Vol. 7, No. 1, pp. 83–87.

Goodlad, J. I. (1984). *A Place Called School: Prospectus for the Future.* New York: McGraw-Hill.

Phi Delta Kappan (September, 1985). *Newsnotes.* Bloomington, Indiana, p. 79.

Phi Delta Kappan (September, 1988). *Research.* Bloomington, Indiana.

Skinner, B. F. (1968). *The Technology of Teaching.* New York, Appleton Century Crofts, p. 22.

Tyler, Ralph (May, 1981). *Curriculum Development Since 1900.* Educational Leadership XXVIII, ASCD, Washington, D.C.

A Nation At Risk: (April, 1985). *The Imperative for Educational Reform.* United States Department of Education, Washington, DC.

Can Corporate America Cope? (November, 1986). *Newsweek.*

CHAPTER 2

CURRENT TRENDS IN STAFF DEVELOPMENT

In pursuit of excellence in education, consideration must be given to the need for creation of excellence in people through the many and varied staff development options now available. Excellence can become a reality if the staff development program focus is upon activities that will truly affect change. This is especially true noting that 85 percent of schools' budgets are designated for salaries. Therefore, it is imperative that school districts become vocal advocates for staff development to protect their financial investment. Educators will continue to need a wide variety of opportunities to grow personally and professionally in order to deliver the best instruction possible for today's children.

With on-going challenges continually confronting education today, providing effective staff development programs has become one of the most unrelenting professional responsibilities for educators. Rapid social, political, and economic change has mandated the need for new knowledge and preparation to teach effectively in the nation's schools.

BASIC ELEMENTS OF STAFF DEVELOPMENT

In the past ten years, major changes have been made in the context, content and environment of staff development. The practices of yesteryear—when a contracted consultant provided one or more presentations of a selected topic to a large group, then departed from the scene, leaving the school district to hope that content would become common practice in the work setting—hopefully are now part of the evolutionary history of staff development. More often than not, nothing happened to the instructional program. This is quite a contrast, when one considers the comprehensive models currently devised and implemented regularly in school districts, which consist of sessions encompassing these steps: (1) awareness, (2) readiness, (3) assessment, (4) staff commitment and in-building planning, (5) implementation, (6) management, (7)

11

refocusing reassessment, (8) evaluation, (9) collaborative efforts, and (10) monitoring student progress. Each of these steps can contribute to an effective staff development program.

Awareness

An initial awareness session is often necessary to provide an overview of proposed program content and to garner participant involvement. This would include the need, history, research, theory, purpose, basic expectations and assumptions concerning the proposed project. Staff then can agree to build shared knowledge and language regarding the program topic. Participants then will read and discuss relevant ideas, concerns, research, and practices. Instruction, expectations, motivation, and discipline dimensions should be considered in relationship to the total school program. Long-term benefits and outcomes are key issues to address during the awareness activities.

Readiness

Readiness often takes considerable time. It cannot be rushed or mandated. It is a sensitive portion of the program since it must permit personnel to become aware of proposed content, and issues and skills necessary to meet program requirements. Personal commitment, reward structure, the decision-making component, and consideration of personal conflicts with existing structures may also be addressed. Timelines, financial and status implications should be outlined in detail. A voting procedure for staff may not be necessary to reach consensus. However, time should be allowed for additional information, discussion, and debate prior to reaching a decision for action. Leadership should be sensitive to concerns of the staff and the need for openly expressing viewpoints concerning renewal and revitalization of programs. The project should be presented to a group of professionals in a way that creates interest, humor, and curiosity. Staff must see the need for change and be active participants in this process.

Staff development programs should not only meet curricular needs, but teacher needs should not be slighted. Too often the importance of the teacher's role in the educational process is overlooked. Dobson and Kessinger (1980) confirm the fact that trainers need to know who teachers are and what they believe. The authors state that, "real improvement in the schooling process will occur when people have a realistic perspective of the relationship between their philosophic stance and their teaching behavior." This concern involves the planning process which must encompass feelings, concerns, and philosophies of teachers.

Needs Assessment

Continuous assessment and problem identification are necessary in order to determine participants' interests regarding the elements of a proposed program. Perceived needs can be identified prior to the selection of an area of work or during process stages. Prioritization is often used to identify a specific area based on demand, sequence of time, or the need for a specific program. Several interactive processes can be used to determine needs and provide for specific prioritized projects. Formal or informal surveys are effective means to assist in formulating ideas, as long as individual and collective responses are surveyed. Discussions are then held to prioritize the survey results. The final refinement of a project can be made by considering the specific objectives listed below:

- to gather accurate information
- to assess what is important to staff
- to collect baseline data to determine program progress
- to set priorities
- to evaluate impact upon a program
- to evaluate strengths and weaknesses
- to monitor program progress
- to identify next steps or sequence.

Staff Commitment/In-Building Planning

Using the committee structure to address in-building needs provides an opportunity for staff ownership, internal involvement, and commitment. The program evolves through a series of work sessions based upon programmatic needs. In addition to the committee structure, it is imperative that provisions be made for frequent interaction with the total staff in order to glean suggestions, keep the program moving ahead, and energize additional enthusiasm for the project. Committee targets include setting goals, objectives, developing an action plan, identifying expected outcomes, establishing time commitments, designing a training plan, identifying the evaluation process, committing necessary resources (human/material), and building an estimated budget. Making the committee's responsibility final must reflect a consensus from staff, superintendent, support service teacher association acceptance, policy review, and a fully informed district school board. Modification and change will, of course, occur, refining the designed process as these various people and agencies react to the proposal.

Implementation

Implementation is the process of launching the plan—making the concept work. It is putting into practice the planned efforts with teachers and students. It is using the steps designed to change behaviors and improve student performance, while writing the practice into school curricula or standard operating procedures. Piloting the program within a controlled situation is the recommended process.

Management

Management involves creating conditions favorable to risk-taking and innovation. It also facilitates organizing, scheduling, and allocating demands on time. Released time, credit, and instructional materials help to stimulate interest. Effects on staff morale, commitment, and staff/student productivity must be considered at all times. Principals should agree openly not to push the staff to panic situations, while teachers should agree to inform principals when there is a lack of synthesis.

Refocusing/Reassessment

The focus on exploration of more universal benefits from the program should not be excluded. One must consider the possibilities of major changes or modifications—seeking ever more effective alternatives. Regularly scheduled seminars, support groups, and peer observations are important. There is an on-going need to regularly stand back, and assess the evolving process and product.

Evaluation

Regular opportunities for reflection are necessary and vital. Evaluation is a continuous process designed to determine the degree to which goals and objectives of the total program are being met. It is on-going, utilizing a variety of approaches and instruments. Sufficient time is needed to implement the practice before actual measurement. Strategies that effect change must be used with a large enough sample in order to gain valid measurement.

Collaborative Efforts

Depending upon the nature and content of the topic of study, carefully selected common interest groups must be identified and involved in the project. Coordination and cooperation with others regarding the proposed program is essential. This effort cannot be overlooked since it can determine the project's ultimate success. These contacts can provide greater involvement of staff, use of diverse expertise, greater visibility, broader communication and perspective, increased acceptance by the school and community, objective evaluation, financial and material support, and better utilization of human resources.

Monitoring Student Progress

Determining the program impact upon student performance obviously is one of the most important aspects of the project. Monitoring the process must be systematically organized by utilizing relevant instruments to gather the necessary data. Specific support information, practical instruments, and simple, efficient record keeping will help to assure accurate measurement of achievement. Monitoring program results can substantiate the need for program continuation or other alternatives. (For specifics, refer to Appendix A.)

THE ADULT LEARNER

If staff development is to become the key provider of knowledge and training for school personnel, the following assumptions are vital:

- An extensive variety of lifetime experiences of the adult learner is brought to the setting which can distort or delay new ideas and concepts relative to preconceived knowledge.
- The vast reservoir of experiences, concepts, attitudes, and knowledge of the adult learner must be recognized and utilized, in order to develop new skills and practices.
- Immediate success and comfortable learning environment can be difficult for the adult to obtain, especially if it represents competition. Group discussion and socialization with others of varied backgrounds and age ranges can minimize these concerns.
- The adult learner's style is more rigid and stabilized, thus making change and acceptance of new and different views more difficult to accept.

- Learning activities based on expressed needs and concerns derived from the participants are preferable.
- Learning takes place more effectively if the climate is informal, respectful and self-diagnosis is utilized.
- Learning is crystallized by a series of satisfactory situations that have a recognized reward system based upon achieving meaningful goals.
- Activities in staff development are viewed in broad terms and the team approach is comforting and reassuring.
- Behavior can be changed with carefully planned long-term orientation, support, a specific sequenced process, reinforcement, guided practice, and follow-up.
- Immediacy of application is important for sustained performance.
- Learning must be persevered as relevant to personal and professional needs.
- Adult developmental tasks increasingly move toward social and occupational role competence and away from more physical developmental tasks.
- A mechanism of mutual help for in-depth planning and evaluation is required.
- A problem-centered orientation to learning is more appropriate.
- Well-organized presentations are preferred using concise, focused format with relevant topics.
- Popular activities tend to be those that are voluntary, self-directed, and self-improvement models.
- Ego involvement may hinder or help the learning process.

In light of the knowledge of the adult learner, each major staff development activity should specifically provide for a range of individual differences, including the following guidelines:

- clear descriptions of expected outcomes using preassessments of needs and interests.
- highly structured activities in small groups with specifically outlined tasks.
- feedback and assistance; regularly reteach and refocus when necessary.
- follow-up activities to ensure mastery.
- provision for alternative practice to meet individual needs and interests.

- learning is enhanced by behavior and inservice that demonstrate respect, trust, and concern for the learner.
- coaching and other assistance to ensure successful implementation.
- continued monitoring, evaluation, encouragement, and reinforcement.

Novice/Experienced Staff

Providing staff development needs for all staff is difficult since individual needs do vary, and using generic content and teaching strategies is not an acceptable practice. There are philosophical considerations necessary for developing effective learning environments. Piaget indicates that the individual in any encounter with environment of necessity organizes the objects and events into existing cognitive structure, and invests them with the meaning dictated by that septum. He/she also perceives each new phenomenon in terms of an already existing conceptual framework.

Teaching strategies for inservice dictate the following sequence: (1) selecting material geared to the learners' state of readiness; (2) instruction for mastery of all learning tasks before new tasks are introduced; (3) providing materials to emphasize sequential learning tasks; (4) utilizing structured learning activities; and (5) guided practice and follow-up practice procedures.

Instructional considerations include established achievement sets, repetition with a context of variety, feedback, successful learning experiences, reinforcement, and active participation.

Factors to consider are:

Pacing. Not everyone learns at the same rate. Staff must be given adequate time to grasp material at hand. Likewise, the participant with a faster learning role should be provided opportunities with challenging or extended activities. Pacing is important to sustain interest and enthusiasm for the content. The objective is to keep the learner on task and confident in the new process.

Learning style. Not everyone learns equally the same way. Learning alternatives should be considered. A humane learning environment is essential throughout the training process; it serves as a model for participants to emulate.

Self-concept. Positive reinforcement and a sense of worth as an individual are important in learning. This is as important with adults as with young students.

Synthetical/analytical. Fragmentation of knowledge is at the root of many educational problems. An integrated approach to learning, in which the recipient recognizes a meaningful relationship among all subjects, is vital.

Self-directed learnings. Participants should learn how they can most effectively discover for themselves the things that are important to them. Once they have "learned how to learn," they become self-directed — choosing their own objectives and meeting them in an effective way — rather than passive receivers of information.

Trust. Participants must know that they can trust the instructor. Learning is more likely to occur in an atmosphere where genuineness and empathetic understanding foster a trusting relationship.

Support. Many, if not most, participants will need strong support in the initial stages. This should gradually be withdrawn (and replaced with another kind of relationship that is more personal and more equal) as the student becomes more independent. (This implies effective observation and follow-up.)

Process. It is in the involvement, in the *doing,* that learning becomes meaningful — not in passive acceptance. The learning process consists of several elements — course material, course structure, individual attitudes, techniques — all of which interact. Each component affects all of the others.

Modular design. It is important that learning activities be self-contained, flexible units, so that instruction can be tailored to the needs of each student.

SELECTING A CONSULTANT

Much has been written about selecting a presenter or consultant to bring about awareness of needed change. Consultants are often referred to as a "kin to a survey." Selecting the right person is the key to success. In making this choice, the following considerations must be made:

- nature and scope of program and outcomes desired.
- consultant's role as a collaborator in problem-solving, a fact finder, a trainer, a technical specialist, a data collector or a reflector.
- understanding of the topic, staff concerns, the approaches to be used, the ability to work well with the identified participants, and with finances.
- reference check.

- conferencing with consultant regarding appropriate program objectives.
- exploring targeted audiences concerning readiness for change.
- potential for working with district personnel.
- establishing a time frame.
- designating specific assignments.
- selecting site, room arrangement, and instructional supplies.

Alternative delivery systems should be available to accommodate participants' diverse learning styles. Follow-up activities may include independent projects designed by the participants for practical use in the classroom. Trainees can implement pilot programs using the consultant's assistance to maintain skills of implementation. Client independence is built after mastery.

A responsible and ethical consultant recognizes and fosters the need for people to develop their own expertise and capabilities. They "Work themselves out of a job" rather than making their trainees dependent on them for continued assistance.

In-House Expertise

There is much in-district expertise that can be utilized in training teams. The essential purpose of any human resource development effort is to increase individual, professional and personal effectiveness and, at the same time, increase organizational effectiveness. Thus, human resource development is equated with growth, both personal and organizational.

Recent research findings and current educational practices have demonstrated efficient use of new learnings in many areas: effective schools, effective teaching, Mastery Learning, classroom management, learning and teaching styles, basic instruction, higher order thinking, study skills, and others. These projects have made a profound change in school climate and, more importantly, in student performance. Knowledge of these practices appears to be worth both the time and effort; thus it becomes necessary for many schools to find ways to incorporate these projects as part of the district-wide staff development programs. In many cases, participants will take control of their own learning. Staff need support persons who take personal responsibility for their own growth and development. They are often pleased to join the ranks of those who want to help others. The staff is usually willing, if provided adequate time and supportive leadership, to develop a series of components that have practical use in the classroom. Staff, by and large, want to become a part of the decision-making process and be on the forefront of change, if provided the opportunity.

Training of Trainers

School districts are encouraging trained classroom teachers to conduct staff development programs. Classroom teachers, as a general rule, prefer to learn from their peers. Many teachers given this responsibility can develop important adult training skills and techniques to become trainers. To develop a trainer of trainers, goals need to be established which will:

- enhance student learning by improving the quality of programs.
- train classroom teachers to conduct staff development programs.
- encourage the use of effective staff development principles (i.e., communication skills, workshop planning, etc.).

Selecting quality participants is an essential factor in obtaining the desired outcomes. The following criteria for participants may be considered in the initial effort. The participant:

- possesses a positive attitude and is open to new learning.
- shows a keen interest in learning.
- has three to five years of teaching experience.
- demonstrates excellence in teaching.
- possesses ability to communicate and work effectively with his/her colleagues.
- is proactive and exemplifies leadership ability.
- exhibits a commitment to personal and professional growth.
- utilizes a balance of race, sex, grade, and subject matter areas in the selective process.

Planning Stage (Phase I)—consists of a thorough orientation where participants become acquainted with an overview of the total program, expected behaviors, and involvement and commitment necessary to become a trainer of trainers. One day is sufficient for this phase.

Training Stage (Phase II)—requires two to three days of comprehensive work addressing the mission, belief system, and scope and sequence of the principles of staff development. Effective preparation and presentation skills should be discussed, modeled, and practiced in great detail.

Content Training Segment (Phase III)—would represent another two-to three-day set of activities where trainers become familiar with the

A TRAINING MODEL

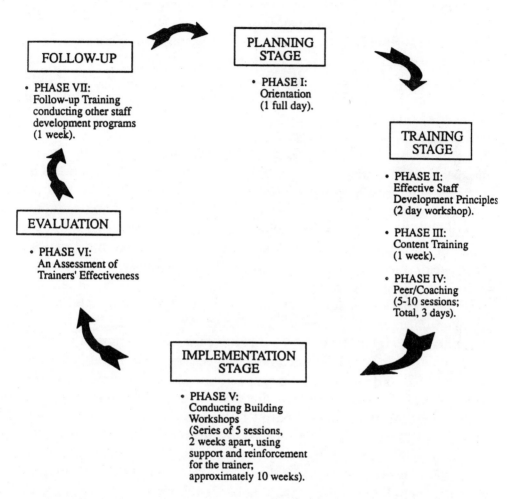

Figure 1. The sequential procedure of the "Training of Trainers" program, outlining the initial steps of the training process.

theory, content, and strategies to be taught. Teams are established to provide support and sharing of ideas.

Coaching (Phase IV)—is an important follow-up segment for the trainers. The comprehensive design of training using interaction at all levels is crucial. On site, follow-up coaching with colleagues, sharing experiences with skill adaptation, and application in classroom practices, provide the trainer with needed support and confidence. This usually requires five to ten sessions.

It is important to make certain that the trainers acquire the necessary knowledge and perfect specific skills which address the behavior or performance before attempting to work with an audience. The trainer's attitude should convey enthusiasm, excitement, and elements of risk taking in order to bring the trainer to the optimal competency level.

There is merit in involving participants in the learning process by making the training a team effort. Joint training ventures, where responsibilities are shared, have the potential of reducing anxiety and providing needed diversity for the participants.

Implementation Stage (Phase V)—is the application stage where participants teach the planned content. Program content and design are important factors when using the Training of Trainers method. The initial content area selected should have universal appeal, in order to attract voluntary and interested participants. This gives the trainer a chance to utilize newly acquired skills with an already-motivated audience. A feeling of success in initial attempts is a major step in training practices. This is extremely important when establishing a working relationship with peers. Teaching peers can pose an anxiety problem, unless the presenter's confidence level is attained early. Peer acceptance and ability to communicate well are essential to success.

Evaluation Stage (Phase VI)—used after each presentation, is an informal process often based on outcomes of objectives. Yearly evaluation can be conducted to determine long-range goals. Questionnaires are useful to assess positive changes in behavior or student performance.

Follow-up and Retraining (Phase VII)—is provided six months or one year after the training, to add new skills, evaluate those used initially, and to extend and advance training techniques. Models of this type can be highly successful if monitored carefully, and if the trainers are provided frequent help and encouragement. Regularly scheduled trainer of trainers meetings should include time to share, discuss, and adapt procedures. Teaching peers requires frequent self-analysis, adjusting instructional techniques and motivational strategies. It is necessary for teachers to be involved in the development and delivery of their own staff development (Snyder & Anderson, 1986). Adult learning experts remind us of the importance of relevance and application to on-the-job problems, as well as the practice of skills in peer teaching (Joyce & Showers, 1982). Success and confidence does not become a reality in the initial training sessions. It requires additional training and practice.

PEER TEACHING/COACHING

The most powerful form of learning and the most sophisticated form of staff development comes not from listening to the "good words" of presenters, but from sharing what we know with others. Learning comes more from giving than receiving, by reflecting on what we do, and by giving it coherence. By sharing and articulating our craft knowledge, we make meaning, we learn (Roland Barth, 1985, p. 93). Collegial coaching is effective when specific strategies or strands are used as a focus. This way the observed teacher learns more about the strategies and becomes more proficient in a variety of skills and techniques.

Staff development can be a means for instructional improvement through peer observation, teaching, or coaching. This provides a cost-effective collegial practice that is personal, professional, and practical. It involves learning, sharing, and growing together. Basic terms in staff development are defined as follows:

- *Peer* —one that is of equal standing with another; a coworker.
- *Coaching* —to train intensively by instruction, demonstration, and practice.
- *Peer Coaching* —Teachers working with other teachers to strengthen a supportive process of observation. Elements of peer coaching are:
  - It is collegial, experimental, and communicative.
  - It is cooperative.
  - It is professional.
  - It is helping.
  - It is trusting.
  - It is confidential.
  - It negates teacher isolation.
  - It contains strategies for team building.
  - It is volunteered after identification.

Peer coaching is classroom-based assistance in which a person skilled in the instructional process assists a coworker in transferring a new skill or strategy into the classroom setting.

The purposes of peer coaching are:

- to provide a framework of sharing of ideas and activities among colleagues and to initiate support for one another.
- to develop a common language and set of understandings.
- to provide a structure for follow-up training, additional activities, acquisition of new skills, and teaching strategies.

The potential for coaching can be a process where the research on teacher effectiveness is fully utilized.

The practice of having teachers watch and provide feedback to one another benefits both the observer and the observed. It provides observation to demonstration, application, and adoptions by first-hand evidence. It promotes risk-taking and growth.

Watching a professionally effective colleague teach can be a valuable experience for both the observer and the one being observed. The following guidelines can alleviate problems as the process unfolds:

- Observation and feedback practices hinge on credibility and trust. One must work with a colleague who can provide support as well as one who shares common interests, mutual respect, and professional concerns.
- A nonjudgmental, nonevaluative posture should be maintained at all times.
- The coaching discussions are confidential and constructive.
- Steps should be taken by the coach to prevent interruptions during the coaching sessions.
- The opportunity to develop a "trust partner" is present. However, there must be freedom to brainstorm new ideas, challenge old ones, discuss successes, frustrations, and challenges.
- Groups of two staff members are teamed to work together.
- Schedules are developed at the convenience of the team members, using the observation time of 20 to 30 minutes as a minimum.
- Team members should consult one another prior to the observation, to decide specifically what it is they want to observe, and to define the focus. It can also be a time to learn the type of lesson planned for the given time frame. Other features can be addressed, such as where to sit, student problems, and class climate.
- The coach spends a good portion of the discussion time in active listening.
- The observer may take nonjudgmental anecdotal notes or script tapes during the observations which relate to only specific practices agreed to in the preconference.
- Postconferences are sharing times for feedback which address the observer's objective reports. The teacher may want to follow up with a self-critique—sharing and discussing plans to exchange roles.

The peer teaching/coaching approach holds promise if the staff development leadership follows their knowledge and experience relative to pairing of human beings in a working setting. Pairings of individuals to accomplish a task must come normally and naturally, not through forced, assigned situations.

Coaching behaviors can be divided into three categories—evaluative, descriptive, and facilitative (Marshall, 1988). Evaluative behavior tells, and to some degree judges good or bad. Descriptive behavior should be valued freely but also used to aid the teacher as a decision-maker. Facilitative behavior asks questions and elicits teacher judgment. It is more open-ended and expands thinking. Getting teachers to talk together is essential and meaningful.

SUMMARY

The trends in staff development are constructive and specific. The following ingredients are included in productive staff development programs:

- The focus should be on the identification of the topic or issue of greatest concern to the professionals who work directly with students.
- A meaningful delivery system should be designed. .
- Consultants should be selected on their ability to relate to the adult learner.
- In-house expertise or local professionals should be used whenever possible.
- Utilization of techniques for cross-fertilization of ideas via trainers and peer-teaching/coaching techniques is a necessity.
- Accountability should be provided by the assessment of results using three sources of data.
- Keeping the total organization—teachers, support services, administration, and board of education—informed is the basis upon which a strong program is continued.

"Staff development" is a professional commitment designed to make the maximum impact upon the greatest number of personnel, who must implement the outcomes of the deliberations. Thus, the careful implementation of the steps outlined this chapter is imperative if success is to be achieved.

REFERENCES

Barth, R. and *Phi Delta Kappan* (December, 1986). *On Sheep and Goats and School Reform.* Bloomington, IN, p. 293.

Billmeyer, Rachel. (1987). Consultant, Coaching Workshop, Omaha Public Schools, Omaha, Nebr.

Blumenfeld, E. and Alpern, L. (1986). The Small Connection: "How to Use Humor in Dealing with People." Englewood Cliffs, NJ: Prentice Hall.

Dillon-Peterson, B. (1981). Staff Development/Organization Development—Perspective 1981. *Staff Development/Organization Development.* Alexandria, VA: Association for Supervision and Curriculum Development.

Dillon-Peterson, B. (1986). Staff Development, A Look into Future. *The Journal of Staff Development,* Vol. 7, No. 1, pp. 124–132.

Dobson, R., Dobson, J. and Kessinger, J. (1980). *Staff Development, A Humanistic Approach.* Washington, DC: University Press of America.

Duncan, M. E., & McCombs, C. (1982). Adult Life Phases: Blueprint for Staff Development Planning. *Community College Review, 10,* 26–35.

Joyce, B. and Showers, B. (October, 1982). "The Coaching of Teaching." *Educational Leadership, 40,* pp. 4–10.

Joyce, B. and Showers, B. (1988). Student Achievement Through Staff Development. New York: Longman.

Joyce, B. and Weil, M. (1986). *Models of Teaching* (3rd ed.). Englewood Cliffs, NJ: Prentice Hall.

Little, J. W. (1981). *School Success and Staff Development. The Role of Staff Development in Urban Desegrated Schools.* Boulder, CO.: Center for Action Research, Inc.

McGowen-Roland, Juanita. (1984). Consultant, Trainer of Trainers Cadre, Omaha Public Schools, Omaha, Nebr.

Naisbitt, J. (1982). *Megatrends.* New York: Warner Books.

Snyder, K. and Anderson, R. (1986). *Managing Productive Schools: Toward an Ecology.* San Diego: Harcourt, Brace, Jovanovich.

Wilsey, C., and Killion, J. (October, 1982). "Making Staff Development Programs That Work." *Educational Leadership, 40,* pp. 36–43.

CHAPTER 3

ORGANIZATIONAL DESIGN FOR STAFF DEVELOPMENT

S taff development represents the life blood of a teaching faculty. The value of staff development activities correlates directly with the degree of involvement of the staff in identifying and selecting the areas and topics to be studied. These activities should be based upon the district's current focus and goals. Regardless of the size of the school system, one person should hold the position of Coordinator of Staff Development and be directly responsible to the Superintendent of Schools. The Coordinator's efforts, in turn, should be articulated with individuals representing the curriculum, staff, and student personnel areas.

A staff development program must be anchored upon the following elements:

- staff development philosophy.
- staff development rationale.
- staff development goals.
- staff development policy.

Philosophy

The school district is committed to the goal of providing quality educational opportunities to the community it serves. To accomplish this goal competent, dedicated personnel are needed to help students achieve their fullest potential.

The staff development program of the school enables personnel to continually grow and expand their ability to facilitate the learning process. The foremost emphasis of any development plan is the notion that training serves to help individual staff members gain new perceptions to foster change. A meaningful staff development program is an integral part of the entire school system; it follows the premise that staff possess a high degree of competency. Development programs are designed to complement that effectiveness.

Staff development enhances the total educational process by combining the personal talents already possessed by individuals with educational experiences to acquire a more proficient fulfilled coalition. The realization of a responsive, meaningful program demands a collaborative effort to offer relevant instructional content. The partnership model is emphasized because it provides a realistic technique which integrates the personal concerns and needs of education professionals for staff development. Resources of the community and from the public school's staff represent great potential for creating learning experiences which help staff provide a richer educational environment for students.

Mission Statement

The purpose of staff development is to provide on-going programs and services designed to explore new developments in education, to assist in the implementation of promising practices, to improve job-related skills, and to foster personal growth of the staff. Staff development is vital for the continued growth and improvement of the school system. It should:

1. enable staff members to grow personally and professionally.
2. provide a means to improve student achievement.
3. offer quality programs.
4. enhance staff morale.
5. provide for communication and sharing among staff members.
6. introduce staff members to new trends and programs.
7. improve the image of the public schools locally and nationally.

Rationale

Education is a lifelong process. In today's fast changing world, everyone needs to be provided with ample and continuing opportunities to develop existing skills while acquiring new ones. Staff development provides an opportunity for public schools employees to grow professionally and personally.

It should be stressed that the ultimate purpose of all programs provided by the school district is to ensure quality educational experiences for students.

The goals of the staff development program are to provide staff members with opportunities to:

1. improve student academic performance and achievement.
2. meet personal and social developmental needs of students.
3. continue improvement of job skills.
4. keep abreast of current developments in their fields of specialization.
5. grow professionally and personally through collaborative internal and external efforts.
6. plan cooperatively, set goals, and exchange ideas among fellow staff members.
7. enhance morale and mental/physical wellness.
8. share successes with colleagues.
9. implement new programs.
10. develop leadership skills.

Board Policy

The Board of Education policy need not be detailed but must clearly give direction, place responsibility for program implementation, and spell out lines of authority. Lines of communication from the staff development program to the Superintendent and Board of Education must be clearly delineated. With a Board policy in place, the structure for program implementation can follow.

The Coordinator must have an organized structure for effective delivery of service. This implies a system for communication with an official Advisory Committee consisting of teachers, administration, and the public. The tenants of a suggested effective organizational, plan includes the specific responsibilities identified below. All the procedural plans must be based upon an adopted Board of Education policy which:

- identifies staff development as a major school district goal.
- recognizes the need for an on-going staff development program in a changing society.
- enables a school system to set up the necessary structure to implement staff development.
- provides funding for staff development activities.
- directs administration to report progress to the Board of Education on a periodic basis as the staff development program progresses.

If the Board of Education policy is to function smoothly, a specific organizational pattern must support the policy statements. Such a plan is outlined in Model II.

Superintendent's Responsibility

The Superintendent of Schools assumes responsibility for the success of the total staff development program as it relates to the Board of Education, staff, and total district. The Superintendent specifically:

- works actively with staff, the Staff Development Coordinator, and building administrators to develop, implement, evaluate, and refine the total staff development program.
- makes resources available to assure success of the program.
- keeps the board of education fully informed relative to staff development activities.
- delegates authority as appropriate, for the smooth delivery of the staff development programs.
- provides positive reinforcement for the total staff development operation.

Principal/Support Staff Role

The principal and support staff should contribute to the staff development program:

- knowledge regarding current educational trends and related research.
- orientation toward concept of continuous learning and improvement.
- understanding of the theories related to learning.
- awareness of programmatic needs.
- utilization of collegial interaction.
- advocacy of quality education for all students.
- ability to translate theory into practice.
- development of a sense of community involving the various publics.
- visionary and risk-taking practices.
- action and orientation to task.
- management of time and resources.
- above all, ability to be creative, yet practical and effective with all students and staff in our changing society.

Responsibilities of the Staff Development Office

The Staff Development Office has responsibility to do the following:

- commit the school system staff to a comprehensive staff development program, working with the Superintendent of Schools.

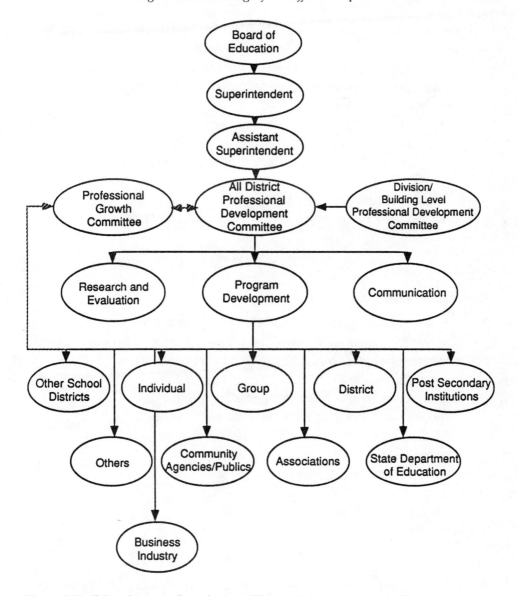

Figure 2. Staff Development Organization. (This model represents a sizable school district. Adjustments must be made to accommodate the individual school system.)

- complete a study of the needs and concerns of staff regarding various activities.
- work with designated building coordinators and department leaders.
- ensure participation is voluntary.
- maintain an in-service resource file.
- study and develop new methods of providing staff development.

- create new and productive relationships by collaborating with post-secondary institutions, the State Department of Education, business and industry, community agencies/publics, other school districts, professional organizations, associations, human-community relations and others.
- ensure that access to the services is easy and equitable and the response for assistance is prompt and efficient.
- work cooperatively with all established committees facilitating the process through initiation, communication, coordination, registration, implementation, and verification.
- develop long range plans that include all department requests.

ADVISORY COMMITTEE

Committee Selection

A. Membership should be selected by utilizing a cross section of employees. Representatives from the following categories could include:
- members of previous staff development committees.
- requests from staff.
- recommendations from teacher association.
- recommendations from other sources.

B. Additional criteria in selecting committee members:
- position.
- subject area.
- competencies.
- college or university representation.
- sex equity.
- tenure.
- race.

C. It is imperative that teachers comprise at least one-half of the committee membership.

D. Appointments should be subject to the superintendent's final approval.

Committee Responsibilities

The responsibilities of the committee are:
To Know:
- comprehensive scope of staff development.
- staff development programs and state/national policies.

- types of "training and development" used by business and industry.
- characteristics of adult learning styles.

To Communicate:

- contents of staff development programs, its revisions and additions.
- building coordinator's responsibilities.
- positive attitude among teachers in pursuing professional growth.
- staff development opportunities available.

To Coordinate:

- services of the local, state and national staff development liaison activities.
- programs that respond to concerns, questions and ideas of staff reported by the building coordinator.
- agenda items of building coordinator's quarterly meetings.

To Plan:

- new methods for staff development programs.
- five year program for staff development.
- new staff development activities using current research.
- timeline procedures.

To Evaluate:

- cadre programs.
- concerns addressed by the Professional Growth Committee.
- staff development proposals.
- delivery of services.
- content and quality of course offerings.

Depending upon the structure and size of the school system, a separate committee may be appropriate to fulfill the personnel office functions regarding acquiring and recording professional growth credits.

Professional Growth Committee

Responsibilities:

- review applications for professional growth.
- initiate professional growth activities to complement individual plans.
- approve individual staff development proposals that necessitate professional growth verification.

- evaluate and validate professional growth activities related to the improvement of instruction.
- assist in the coordination of the staff development policies and procedures.

Building Coordinators

Responsibilities:

- represent the interests of the staff at the building level.
- become familiar with the philosophy, plans, and procedures for staff development identified in the staff development program.
- provide information about the program to all staff and assist with enrollment procedures.
- serve as the liaison between the school and the staff development office.
- work with the building administrator(s) to plan effective inservice programs that correlate with the school's goals and objectives.
- attend quarterly meetings schedules with the Staff Development Committee.
- keep building notebooks current and disseminate materials to staff.
- deal with concerns of staff by communicating with building principal, and others in the supervisory role.
- help facilitate the delivery of staff development service with ease and efficiency.
- become a resource person to improve the staff development processes.
- submit articles to be published in the "Staff Development" publication.

Individual Staff Members

Responsibilities:

- become knowledgeable with the contents of the staff development program.
- formulate a plan that will help achieve desired goals and objectives.
- review the basic requirements for professional growth.
- consult with other grade level of subject area teachers, subject area supervisor, or immediate superior to discuss areas of interest/need.
- cooperatively plan experiences that will address objectives.
- utilize the course description segment to select courses and other activities.
- complete and submit the registration form prior to the beginning of the course.

- participate in the growth experience by preparation, attendance, involvement, and application.
- know the number of credits earned and the number needed to meet professional growth requirements.

The entire school district plays a major role in the success of the staff development programs and services.

Most school districts have a plan for professional development. These plans are usually of one year duration. However, some are projected for a limited number of years into future school semesters. The plans are designed to assist with achieving short-range as well as long-range goals. Planning provides a means for staff to look ahead and organize activities in a systematic fashion. The annual plan breaks the long-range extended plan into achievable short-range goals. Both are needed: Long-range planning provides perspective, while the annual plan is a manageable entity.

Purposes of the professional development plan:

- provides a means for personal and professional planning.
- aids in long-range planning of goals and objectives.
- assists compliance with state statute for professional growth requirements.
- establishes an informal needs assessment for the staff development office.
- facilitates cooperative planning with administrators.
- provides evaluation.

INCENTIVES AND REWARDS

Rewarding school personnel for staff development activities poses a genuine challenge. Monetary rewards, per se, can create serious fiscal burdens upon school districts. Consequently, innovative approaches must be designed to reward staff. Schools have utilized a variety of methods to ensure fair and equitable procedures to reward participating staff members.

Some of the identified procedures include the following:

- *released time for staff development activities.* Coverage is usually provided by paid substitute teachers.
- *inservice as part of the professionals contractual obligation.* The inservice program becomes part of the ongoing school term.

- *specific stipends paid on an hourly basis for participation in a specific staff development activity.* These stipends do not become part of a teacher's base salary.
- professional growth points are recorded on a professional growth form which enhances career advancement.
- *nonmonetary incentives.* These incentives include a vast number of recognitions ranging from the awarding of certificates, recognition luncheons, including names in reports to the board of education, to allowing personnel to attend selected conferences at board of education expense. The key to incentives and rewards is overt recognition of the professional for a job well done.

Community Role

Responsibilities:

- identify specific elements of problems which can encompass a wide spectrum of issues.
- select representative personnel with knowledge, interest, and means to address the topic.
- design a cooperative plan to explore, study, and research the given topic.
- define the parameters of the topic to achieve the desired outcome.
- clarify the roll of the participants as advisors in achieving the possible solutions to the identified problem.
- indicate that at the termination of the study the Advisory Committee will be dissolved.

Depending upon the structure and size of the school system, a separate committee may be appropriate to fulfill the personnel office functions regarding acquiring and recording professional growth credits.

Staff development represents a significant investment in professional time, money, and new ideas. It is imperative that a carefully designed comprehensive structure exists to assure that the topic being studied is in a framework of orderliness and efficiency. The suggestions in this chapter should help in guaranteeing sound organizational design.

REFERENCES

Bey, T. M. (July, 1986). *CPR A Model for Effective Goal Setting.* Washington, D.C., Eric Clearinghouse on Teacher Education, No. SP 27312.

Crandall, D. P. and Associates. (1982). *People, Policies and Practices Examining the Chain of School Improvement.* Andover, MA: The Network.

Dillon-Peterson, B. (1986). Staff Development, A Look into Future. *The Journal of Staff Development,* Vol. 7, No. 1, pp. 124–132.

Glickman, C. D. (1985). The Supervisor's Challenge: Changing the Teacher's Work Environment. *Educational Leadership,* Vol. 42, No. 4, pp. 39–40

Good, T. L. and Brophy, J. E. (1974). *Teacher-Student Relationships.* New York: Holt, Rinehart & Winston, Inc.

Loucks, S. F. and Pratt, H. (1979). Effective Curriculum Change Through a Concern-based Approach to Planning and Staff Development. *Educational Leadership,* Vol. 37, No. 3, pp. 212–215.

McCombs, B. (1984). Processes and Skills Underlying Continuing Intrinsic Motivation to Learn: Toward a Definition of Motivation Skills Training Interventions. *Education Psychologist,* Vol. 19, No. 4, pp. 199–218

Sparks, G. M. (1983). Synthesis of Research on Staff Development for Effective Teaching. *Educational Leadership,* Vol. 41, No. 3, pp. 65–72.

CHAPTER 4

PLANNING, DELIVERY OF STAFF DEVELOPMENT

The genesis to all successful inservice activity is the ability of the Staff Development Coordinator and faculty to identify the genuine areas of professional need of the staff, in order to promote these projects and activities, which are vital to the mission of the school system. This is an important element in the total staff development process. Identification of staff needs is an ongoing process, targeting both long- and short-range objectives. It is also important to remember that leadership must be able to discriminate between "wants" and "needs." "Wants" might fall into the category of fulfilling a marginal interest or desire; a "need" should represent addressing basic shortcomings in one's training and experience. Herein lies the secret of the importance of making a careful and complete evaluation of staff needs. These objectives can be fulfilled if the coordinator involves faculty at all stages of the planning process.

NEEDS ASSESSMENT

Purpose

The needs assessment process is an extremely important segment since it provides the school district with accurate information to use in making effective decisions regarding staff development programs. It also serves as a means to assess the thinking of individual staff members. Assessment allows staff to set priorities and justifies focusing attention on some things and not on others. Staff may become more sensitive to what they are doing when provided with an opportunity to complete an assessment, thus assisting them in evaluating programmatic strengths and weaknesses. The assessment can also provide priority direction and sequencing.

Methods

There are various methods that can be used to assess staff contributions, both formal and informal. They are as follows:

- analyzing existing documents, tests, prior needs assessments, records *memos*, budgets, goal statements, staff development proposals, and others.
- studying standardized test results, utilizing previous needs assessment data, considering budgetary and department goal statements, reviewing staff development proposals, and evaluating self-study recommendations, both external and internal.
- utilizing observations or interviews (structured or unstructured), surveys, and questionnaires.
- reviewing participatory strategies, group discussions, and evaluations from course offerings, conference and workshop programs.
- reviewing recommendations from the Board of Education, superintendent, building administrators, and other support staff.
- consideration of current research.

Having conscientiously followed the procedures identified above, specific plans for delivery can be established. Vagueness ("what are we trying to do," and "who is going to do what") will be avoided if the above elements of the planning process are in place.

A staff development project geared to the genuine needs of a given group of people, and implemented by persons who are knowledgeable concerning these needs, is the key to a successful program. The thesis must be stressed again and again: Planning, and more planning, of every detail is essential in the total staff development process.

Outside groups and agencies must be identified carefully. Some criteria to be followed in their selection include:

- a general feeling that the group/agency will tend to be constructive in furthering the course of the project.
- the group/agency's philosophy relative to the topic must be considered.
- willingness of the outside constituencies to abide by the boundaries of the specific project is paramount.

After the needs assessment results are finalized, the identification of specific areas of need should bring staff to the threshold of considering purpose of the program or activity. Would the purpose be:

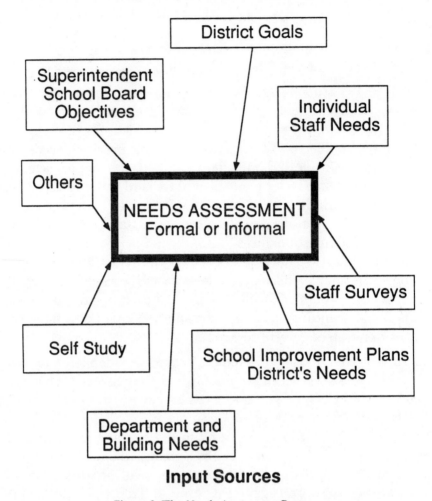

Input Sources

Figure 3. The Needs Assessment Process.

- development of a new program or segment of a program?
- extension of knowledge and skills?
- acquisition of new teaching techniques or strategies?
- shaping of attitudes and purpose (change process)?

Staff must seek the most effective route for the delivery of district or building staff development. It should be noted that creative ideas for problem solution may come from professionals as well as interested laypersons. It depends on the demand or district decision. The program offering may be a district-wide program for all schools, a cluster of schools, an individual building, or a single course offering or workshop series offered to those who wish to participate.

In any individual building program, the principal must be committed to provide the necessary leadership to carry out the program delivery that best meets the needs of the staff. In planning programs, whether district-directed or building-initiated, the following considerations are necessary:

- district and specific building objectives.
- staff needs and practicality of proposed activity.
- concerns expressed via surveys by community advisory and self-study committees.
- availability of personnel to provide programs.
- timelines necessary for effective programs.
- efforts to facilitate growth and change.

The first step in the planning sessions should be the identification of the core or program area to be addressed. The committee members should consist of those staff that are responsible for the specific areas. The second step would deal with the planning steps would mean exploring the availability of quality services and resources and determining which of these would be the most relevant for the stated needs. The Staff Development Coordinator can be most helpful with rap sessions, program planning, and action steps. The building leadership should obtain permission and support from the central office prior to proceeding.

Obtaining information from the central office, State Department of Education, University, and other available areas with useful information often provides a variety of options to consider. Once the plan has taken shape, the building administrator and other support personnel become responsible for the initial action steps of the plan. Staff members, too, assume responsibility for the program, training, implementation, and monitoring.

Guidelines

Timing is important, since the information gathered should be used in such a manner that the respondents feel ownership in the feedback, and are a part of the action taken as a result of the gathered data. Attention should be focused to obtain information from the respondents about *how* they learn as much as *what* they want to learn.

Staff Involvement

Staff development awareness sessions help participants to identify areas of interest which can serve as springboards to provide follow-up services and designing of courses to respond to stated needs. Staff should be provided sessions using activities where they can identify strengths and competencies, thus giving staff development leadership a means to identify instructors or group leaders. Peer observations and coaching techniques will often give rise to expressed needs for activities. Staff appreciate sessions designed to allow for sharing ideas, resources, and needs.

Process

Designing the instrument is possibly the most time-consuming and arduous task of the assessment process. Great care must be given to the choice of topics, semantics, form, length, quality, and composition. The assessment procedure is best achieved by forming a working committee consisting of a cross-representation of staff, where all departments can have a voice in the formation of the instrument. The purposes, composition, and form must be agreed upon as a first step. The topic areas and questions are basic and will require much deliberation, since the instrument should be concise and at the same time comprehensive enough to cover the diversity of staff. Preliminary drafts should be reviewed by a steering committee or immediate supervisors. Support personnel can be helpful with editing, for refinement and inclusiveness. The instrument is then administered to staff; results consolidated, interpreted, and prioritized for analysis.

PROGRAM IDENTIFICATION/SETTING OF OBJECTIVES

Once "needs" have been identified, the obvious question has to be answered: How is the identified area going to be developed? The "how" deals with formulation of specific objectives related to the area of study. Objectives can become an end rather than a means to an end. If one knows what is wanted, objectives can be stated briefly, specifically, and concisely. Verbose, run-on objectives should be avoided, because a set of objectives is the map for successful completion of the proposed project. Finally, objectives formulated for the specific project must correlate with the overall district goals and be attainable.

SPECIFIC PLAN FOR DELIVERY

In-depth planning is the key to successful delivery of any staff development program. No stone can be left unturned in preparing for such a project. All phases of the program must be complete in every detail, and the parts must mesh to represent a comprehensive whole. People, the "right people," represent the keys to success. In this "people" dimension, consideration must be given to:

- involvement of "target" staff.
- selection of staff representing support areas.
- selecting outside agencies and groups for resources and advisory assistance.

Specifically, the targeted staff should be those persons who helped in the identification of the area of study. Usually, these persons will be classroom teachers. Support staff, generally representing administrative and supervisory personnel, can include department chairs, counselors, lead teachers, etc. They should be involved as partners and active participants in the study. They can help to initiate action and sustain the program.

If all procedures of the proposed project discussed in this chapter are implemented with care, a successful staff development project should be well underway.

DELIVERY OF PLANNED INSERVICE

Learning is not a spectator sport. Thus, the acquiring of knowledge, perfecting professional skills and developing positive attitudes is the ultimate objective of inservice education. If the planning phase of inservice education is being painstakingly implemented, meaningful learning will become a reality.

Specifically, this means that:

- staff development activities do indeed reflect the assessed needs of participants.
- the activities focus upon the setting in which staff do their job.
- the activities allow for specific skill development.
- activities are flexible and can be modified over a period of a few years.
- last, but not least, the activities have the approval, support and

involvement of all levels of administration, including the local board of education.

Program delivery is the product of carefully designed sequential, developmental steps. Content is geared toward a specific grade level, a specific topic, and a specific set of skills.

Prescription

Prescription is the determination of *what*, and *how*, the identified area of content should be delivered. The selection of theory, instructional strategies, grouping of personnel, specific assignments, and identifying related activities are all integral parts of prescribing the operational activities of the content area. Once again, planning to the last detail is essential.

Presentation of Theory

"Theory" is, according to the dictionary, "an explanation based on thought, observation and reasoning." This implies utilizing current research, reporting recent trends and reviewing current literature. Theory should be utilized only to reinforce clear and immediately useful points. Theory should support the area of content under consideration; it should project further developments in the field and the possible directions for change. Theory is an integral part of the delivery system, not its end.

Modeling/Demonstration of Skills

The skillful teacher varies the delivery systems. The greater the number of skills, the greater the chances for holding the attention of the participating group. The instructor must serve as an example for the learners. Suggested variations, among others, would include the classic lecture—not too lengthy—as well as demonstrations, discussions, role playing, inquiry, and use of teaching aids. The delivery techniques used must fit the stated objectives. The delivery techniques used must fit the stated objectives, without wandering too far from the identified goals. The completed presentation should be a model which can be utilized by the teacher in the classroom setting. If this transfer can be completed, the instruction has been successful.

Practice Under Simulated Conditions

Opportunity to practice a new skill is imperative for behavior change (Brophy & Good, 1974.) Role playing is effective and is a meaningful way to practice a skill and, incidentally, can provide fun in learning. Staff development works best when individuals get a chance to participate in demonstrations, supervised tasks and receive constructive criticism. Often the guided practice segment can provide the necessary confidence and encouragement that the adult learner needs to effect change. Techniques used must fit stated objectives and must be such that participants can transfer the use of the demonstrated procedures with students.

Structured Feedback

Professional development activities in which participants share and help each other are more likely to attain the objectives of the inservice project than those in which participants work alone. Instructors must be open with well-deserved praise for genuine effort and achievement. Positive reinforcement for good responses, constructive attitude, and signs of behavioral changes are of prime importance. This positive feedback needs to be given quickly to emphasize achievement and, if necessary, to avoid repetition of mistakes, all of which add up to improved performance. Adults, like children, need affirmation regarding the task performed.

Coaching for Application

Coaching is the occasional presence in the classroom of another adult who has considerable knowledge of the content under discussion. It appears to be a recognized powerful means for teachers to learn complex new practices. Coaching can also provide valuable support and peer assistance, which is often necessary for classroom teachers who are willing to try new learned skills to improve their teaching. This transition of skill development is a valuable component of staff development.

Monitoring for Success

The art of good teaching includes effective monitoring of student performance at all age levels, including the adult learner. The instructor must check to see if participants can complete and actually are working on designated tasks. Methods utilized are many and varied, including observation, checking work, answering questions and general discussion.

Monitoring provides a basis for diagnosis. It is especially important because it should provide the instructor with information to decide upon the next instructional step. This information can lead to more feedback, additional presentations, re-teaching, and revised diagnosis and prescription. This individual contact with the participants improves climate, acceptance, and insures accountability.

Effective implementation of any staff development project includes for major categories. These are:

Category I — Awareness.

In this category, the major questions to be answered are, *"What is it?"* *"What* can it do for me?"

What area has been identified to be studied or researched? Unless personnel understand clearly what is being targeted for study and what it can do for them, all will be lost.

Category II — Process.

In the "process" category, the procedure — namely the specific steps to be taken in the study — are identified and clearly explained. The "how we are to proceed" is clearly delineated. "Where do we start?" and "How far do we go?" are questions which are answered.

Category III — Implementation.

The implementation step initially represents the "try it out" stage. Teachers must try out the suggested procedures or plan. In one sense, this is the "dry run." Does it work in my classroom? Do the children and I feel comfortable with the plan? Does it improve student performance? If the "dry run" doesn't live up to expectations, it can be withdrawn or modified without the label of "failure" of a given project. If the program meets the test, then the project can be fully implemented.

Category IV — Internalization — Actualization.

The proof of the "pudding" is in the utilization of the material learned. If indeed the first three categories have measured up to expectations, then the results of the inservice can be incorporated into the program. The degree of success can be measured by the extent to which teachers, administrators and the other professionals involved, have accepted the program, made it work, and are identifying with the elements of the project. Once the point has been reached where professionals can say, "This is *my* program," personalization has been achieved.

A CAUTION

In the larger picture, it is always essential to consider how the given project fits into the total curriculum. With the advent of dozens of "packaged programs" on the market, plus staff development activities often focused upon some learning model, the curriculum can suffer from fragmentation. The following "Staff Development Services Model" identifies the factors which need to be considered when contemplating a study. These factors might well be considered to be a "frame of reality" within which each school district must work. Too, the model shows how all parts of a staff development and program interlock to establish a sound comprehensive curriculum.

SCHEDULING AND ORGANIZATION

Time

Staff development is a year-round activity and should not be a structured two-semester plan, but open for proposals and district-wide activities throughout the year. Many school districts create a course catalog in the fall and add new courses each month, in addition to major district-wide programs. Fall is appropriate since the opening of school gives rise to new learning and new opportunities. Late spring is a winding-down time, making it difficult to attract participants.

Evening sessions after school are not popular, but depend on district precedent and what is necessary. Saturday sessions are of low priority unless stipends are available. Summer is an excellent time if stipends can be used to attract targeted staff. This allows for a series of classes, addressing a specific topic and where skill development can be a reality. Dinner meetings are costly, but appropriate and popular in some areas.

Planning staff development should be an essential part of master calendar planning, with days made available for staff meetings and other association events. If a specific time is set aside, one must avoid tentative dates and changes when other events appear. It is difficult to please everyone. Staff development activities should have high priority and be scheduled in a series, at least a week or two apart.

Release Time

Release time is probably the most desirable means to provide continuing education for staff. However, with budget constraints and respect for the continuity of learning for students, this is not practiced often. Many districts have tried a staff development day every month or once a quarter/semester. The practice of starting school late or letting students leave early is popular especially where student transportation is a problem. Legislatures are now looking at extended contracts as a feasible way to address this concern. This would mean staff would have one or two weeks after school ends, or would begin early in the fall.

Rewards

Staff development growth points are popular means to get staff to become involved. Many states have laws requiring a specific number of points in three to five years in order to keep certification valid. There are several ways to approach this. Courses can be classified into sections and the requirements would pertain to specific numbers.

Certificates are popular as an achievement reward. There are, of course, many staff members interested in the knowledge and skills. They do not require any reward and prefer the intrinsic value of the course.

Multi-Level Input

Regardless of how broad and comprehensive the overall staff development offering may be, program quality is measured not by quantity of offerings, but rather by meeting grass-roots needs. Time and energy must target upon requests which come from individuals, coordinators, teachers, and principals who have identified the areas, problems or topics of concern which these people feel will result in an improved program for children. To achieve the goal of identifying these personalized topics, procedures must be developed which will provide mechanisms for bringing these requests to the fore.

The "proposal form" (Appendix A) plan can serve as a valuable means for staff to develop their own inservice or program requests. This plan insures ownership and responsibility for implementation. When staff can identify and write objectives while designing their own activities the relevant aspects are most evident. Buildings, departments and other divisions have needs for specific programs and often prefer to develop their own projects.

If the school district so decides, these proposed courses can be disseminated into a current course guide, where registration may be a means for other staff to become involved. The form should include the objectives or purpose and brief description of the offering accompanied by the time, place, date, clock hours, instructor, and signature of principal, supervisor, or department chairman. The proposal then is approved by central office personnel. The "proposal form" can be successful if all requests are given consideration, study, and support. Each principle must be judged on its own merit and its relationship to approved district goals.

Spin-Off

It has been stated that staff development is a never-ending process. Linkages develop as the process proceeds. The completion of one topic, almost without fail, opens a new vista for study. A unit dealing with children's achievement, for example, leads to principles of child development, setting goals and objectives, testing, and so on.

Spin-off is a valuable dimension, which can represent professional growth and the evolutionary process for a school which has become change oriented via a constructive staff development program.

REFERENCES

Fielding, G. D. and Schalock, H. D. (1985). *Promoting the Professional Development of Teachers and Administrators.* Eugene, OR: University of Oregon.

Good, T. and Brophy, J. E. (1974). *Teacher-Student Relationships.* New York: Holt, Rinehart and Winston, Inc.

Huberman, A. and Miles M. et al. (1982). *Innovation Up Close: A Field Study in Twelve School Settings.* Andover, MA: The Network.

Johnson, D. and R. Johnson. (1983). *Learning Together and Alone.* Englewood Cliffs, NJ: Prentice Hall.

Jones, L. L. and Hayes, A. E. (1980). How Valid are Surveys of Teacher Needs? *Educational Leadership,* Vol. 37, pp. 390–392.

McGregor, D. (1960). *The Human Side of Enterprise.* New York: McGraw Hill.

Wood, F. W. and McQuarrie, F. O. (1984). The Missing Link: A Process to Select and Implement the Recommendations. *Journal of Staff Development,* Vol. 5, No. 2, pp. 57–64.

CHAPTER 5

IMPLEMENTATION: KEY ELEMENT

Implementing the results of a staff development project involve many considerations. Key questions which must be answered objectively are:

- will the project increase the knowledge and skills of the professionals, teachers, principals and coordinators to better serve students?
- will the project, directly or indirectly, have a positive effect upon student performance?
- does the project hold promise for a long-range effect upon the curriculum or training objective?
- what mechanisms are needed for sustaining interest in the project?

THE PROFESSIONAL'S KNOWLEDGE AND SKILLS

The professional is an adult learner. All the rules of working with adult learners must be kept in mind. These rules range from selecting the "right topic" to developing mechanisms for breaking down participation barriers. Only as the participants begin to internalize the importance of the activity can one hope for positive effect upon student performance.

Student Performance

Having accepted the value of the content of the project, the professional must reflect upon ways and means to share this knowledge with students. The greater the degree of acceptance and interest in the given project, the easier it will be for the teacher to employ her/his teaching strategies to inculcate the new material.

Long-Range Promise

Only as the professional sees the linkages with other areas of the curriculum, and conveys this to the learners, will there be hope of long-range effect upon children. The danger of isolated segments of information rising and falling with the current whims of the moment must be taken for what they are worth, and not at the expense of valuable participant time.

Sustaining the Effort

Implementing a new staff development program requires a high degree of effort from all participants. It is far more important than attending a series of workshops, returning to the work arena, and implementing the program. Designing training sessions that provide the real "cement" is the challenge which must be systematically addressed.

Staff are naturally more influenced by their own backgrounds, interests, and experiences. Their perceptions of students' interests and abilities are more important to them than information from other sources. Therefore, professional working relationships must first be established. Time for this process is an important initial step. Professional competencies and specific skills of staff need to be identified. This can be accomplished via group study and planning sessions.

A school-wide change effort should come from the staff. Knowledge of this planned change must follow evenly and with focus on the desired outcomes. The proposed innovations may appear frightening and overwhelming for the majority of staff who see them as complex, demanding, and a threat to former teaching strategies.

Information sharing between teachers from different departments, teams, or grade levels makes for a successful implementation process. The school administrative team is a vital link and should be a part of the initial training, organizing, and sharing activities. Open, constructive, nonjudgmental dialogue is essential. Voluntary participation of staff is a contributing factor to success. This does not mean that recruitment and selling the program to others is prohibited. All should be a part of the decision-making process as well as the selection and organization of the training segments. Social interaction is the dominant mode of educational change.

Key factors that are beneficial in sustaining an effective program are:

- relevance of program, staff-initiated programs, with long-range objectives.
- carefully selected representative committees to assume specific responsibilities to facilitate program follow-through.
- plans that involve staff and empower teachers to work together.

- a risk-taking atmosphere where the effects of change can be discussed openly, honestly, with provision for staff input.
- analysis of needs, resources, and concerns addressed periodically.
- support groups established to provide feedback.
- social interaction to alleviate stress, build self-esteem, and let staff legitimate involvement.
- goal-setting sessions to comply with time lines, resources, and practicality.
- continuous training for teachers designed by teachers to update and reinforce segments of learning with emphasis on teacher skills and knowledge.
- actual working involvement of the administrative teams, superintendent, supervisors, principals, support staff.
- released time for faculty to plan, work together, training and evaluation of outcomes.

EFFECTING REAL CHANGE

Real changes in program are based upon solid conceptualization, has substance and can be implemented within the given school or school system. The ultimate objective of improving student performance must be constantly in the forefront.

Consequently, consideration must be given to the following:

- Identifiable measurable desired outcomes must be established (behavior change expected).
- There is periodic evaluation of student performance (mastery tests-paper, observational, discussion).
- There is reinforcement of knowledge and teaching strategies for staff.
- Systematic goals are verbalized and reiterated to provide on-going support at all organizational levels. (Special area teachers, supervisors, etc.)
- There is evidence of a high degree of self-expectations and commitment on the part of both teachers and students. (All are ready to act.)
- Immediate implementation and feedback of skills learned must be an accepted procedure. (Try out the idea as soon as possible.)

- Multiple options must be available for topic implementations. (The teacher utilizes a variety of teaching strategies.)
- Success is evident in teacher and student performance. (The teacher is demonstrating new approaches and students are motivated.)
- Resources and training needs are available when needed (hardware, software, and a variety of special materials are available).
- Team effort is an integral part of the process. (Teachers, students and support staff represent a total school effort.)

NECESSARY SUPPORT MECHANISMS

Staff development activities, if well conceived according to the various guidelines proposed in this study, demand a major commitment of time, effort and energy from professional personnel. Thus, the responsibility for careful planning of a staff development project must transcend programmatic considerations. Many contributing factors can and will have a significant impact upon the proposed project.

Time

Time represents money, and is extremely valuable, particularly when considered in the context of a professional who is responsible for the learning experiences of a sizable group of children. "Time on Task" is an important dimension in the learning process. The school with a good record of time spent upon instruction, with minimal interruptions, tends to be a school not only with significant scholastic accomplishments, but also a school with a high degree of good school climate. The nebulous ingredient, hard to measure but vital to success, is evidence of a warm, friendly learning environment.

Consequently, there probably is no "right" or "best" time for scheduling staff development meetings. Each project must be scheduled individually and time needed must be projected conservatively. Gone should be the days when curriculum and instructional development projects were conducted immediately "after school" with little or no break, thus representing a continuation of the school day which, in some cases, began at 8:00 a.m.

Suggested procedures to improve upon are:

- after school . . . sessions may work if refreshments, diversity in program activities, and adequate work environment are provided.

- a series of meetings held approximately once a month apart, allowing time for staff members to pilot the learning techniques in the classrooms, has proven highly successful.
- two or three full-day sessions held at a site apart from the school setting usually prove to be a wise investment of time and resources. This plan, however, calls for a well-structured agenda allowing time for interaction among participants.
- special committee/groups with specific assignments can meet at their convenience over and above the assigned meeting times to accomplish their objectives toward program implementation.
- the ideal time segment is the extended school year, whereby staff can have two weeks before the opening or after closing of the school year.
- some school districts have designated staff development days as one day per month, every two or three months, or each quarter.

Staff development must now be considered as a year around activity. Leadership should think in terms of a time frame of 12 months in order to implement a total staff development program. The modern staff development program gives specific attention to released time for teachers.

Released Time for Teachers

The following concepts are important to released time for teachers so that they may participate in staff development:

- When and how much time should be scheduled so that continuity of learning for children should not be greatly interrupted.
- The mode of providing effective coverage for teachers if absence from classroom is a necessary consideration.
- Use can be made of holidays and summer, adopting the extended contract concept.
- Consider the reward systems for professionals, both intrinsic and extrinsic, in the form of professional growth points, certificates, stipends, and college credit.
- The role of administrators at all levels in reinforcement of constructive projects is of vital importance.
- The synergistic effect of constructive growth, in areas such as problem solving and inductive teaching techniques, can lead to improved student achievement and eventually to higher complex thinking skills.

Team Effort

There is no substitute for team work. Good teachers do not isolate themselves and run a one-person show. When philosophies spread a broad spectrum within the team, successful teachers seek some area of compatibility in which to share, expand, and carry the group ahead to higher thinking levels.

Receptivity for Realistic Change

The implementation process should allow openness to the extent that new ideas will be tried to the fullest. Yet, not forgetting or attempting to change the well founded successful procedures. Obviously, discarding obsolete or unsuccessful strategies is an important facet to realistic change.

REINFORCEMENT

Keeping staff on task and accepting the discomforts of realistic change will require continual reinforcement from the administration, coworkers, and support staff. It is essential that teachers develop a philosophical acceptance of new practices through knowledge of research and a rationale for effectiveness of the techniques. Staff must be able to express doubts and object openly to the practicality of the proposed practice. This, however, is done more effectively in small groups where those who feel the need to resist can do so. Seeing, hearing, and experiencing are processes characteristic of innovation. Staff expressions of doubt and confusion reveal signs of learning, and can be helped by those who are convinced that the practice is workable. Testimonies of effectiveness and usefulness should be the basis for peer discussions.

Recognition of the interrelatedness of skills will help teachers to build confidence, provide direction and establish credibility. Teachers need to support one another, use preliminary coaching techniques, and encourage administrators and support staff to serve as positive reinforcers and sounding boards for the challenge at hand.

Transformation

Changes which have been implemented and have been in operation for a considerable period of time have, in essence, proved themselves and tend to be accepted. These changes have, in many instances, made a positive impact upon staff and students.

As a result of a quality staff development program, the consumers have grown professionally and are making strong efforts to implement new and additional effective program segments. As these effective segments are implemented, additional growth is a spin-off and thus continues the upward learning spiral. New frontiers of information also can open up, horizons are expanded, and the professionals are operating upon a higher level of competence.

Innovations can succeed if administrators and staff aim high, remain persistent, and work and learn together for the purpose of linking all facets of the program. Commitment is essential to success. Assistance and timing constitute vital ingredients for continuity and continuation. Mastery of the innovation remains the major outcome. It is evident that mutual support and staff development are inseparable. Thus, if these elements are indeed present, transformation is now a reality!

REFERENCES

Bolster, A. S. (1983). "Toward a More Effective Model of Research on Teaching." Harvard Educational Review, p. 53.

Elliott, E. (Ed.) (1985). *Learning and Teaching the Ways of Knowing.* Eighty-fourth Yearbook of the National Society for the Study of Education, Part II. Chicago: University of Chicago Press.

Fielding, G. D. and Schalock, H. D. (1985). Promoting the Professional Development of Teachers and Administrators. Eugene, OR: University of Oregon.

Little, J. W. (1981). School Success and Staff Development: The Role of Staff Development in Urban Desegregated Schools. *Executive Summary.* Washington DC: National Institute of Education.

Luberman, A. and Miller, T. (1984). *Teachers, Their World and Their Work: Implications for School Improvment.* Alexandia, VA: Association of Supervision and Curriculum Development.

Stallings, J. (1981). "Changing Teacher Behavior: A Challenge for the Eighties." Paper delivered at the American Education Research Association, Los Angeles, CA.

CHAPTER 6

RELATIONSHIPS FOR SUCCESS

S taff development is a central function of a school district. Inherent in this responsibility is the recognition that staff development does not operate in isolation. If the promise of American education is to be fulfilled, many gaps must be bridged between the school district and the various communities which the school represents. A sampling of community agencies would include minority groups, various special interest groups, local businesses, institutions of higher education, state governmental agencies, such as the Department of Education and, of course, industry. The listing could go on and on.

Collaborative effort is the keystone to success when working with personnel outside the formal school structure. The staff development task for which community involvement has been solicited must represent a mutually beneficial activity. It is indeed a challenge of the first order to so structure a project so that all participants feel that they are contributing, and that it is a benefit to all persons involved.

One major key to genuine collaborative effort rests in bringing together the right "mix" of people for the proposed project. The answer in involvement rests not in the across-the-board selection of large numbers of people; rather, success lies in assessing which individuals or groups can make the most significant contribution to the identified project.

If selection of personnel is a key element for collaborative activity, then concern must be with personal and professional growth of all participants. The elements which represent personal and professional growth are many and varied. Basically, they include training in leadership and planning skills for the purpose of implementing staff development programs within a given school or school district. These programs will be directed primarily toward one or more of the five groups: teachers, administrators, resource support, and noncertified personnel. Yet, the training and growth must equally be reflected in the selected group who are an integral part of the project under consideration.

Collaboration activities can include one or more of the following:

- consulting with other schools, local agencies, and specific departments concerning specialized training programs.
- engaging in coordinating and planning meetings with representative groups.
- organizing trainers-of-training segments for specific teams of personnel.
- conducting of special inservice activities addressing such topics as instructional leadership, supervision of instruction, parenting, development of greater cultural awareness, classroom management, and furthering interpersonal relationships.

COMMUNITY SERVICE AGENCIES

In every school community there are numerous community service agencies which are willing and able to share valuable expertise. In many cases, they are available to cooperatively plan specific programs of services for staff, students, and other selected participants. These organizations are vital links in the collaborative process. Utilizing the talents and organizational segments already in place, a stable, viable program that can address current societal problems and be a forum for continuous learning, can become a reality.

STATE DEPARTMENT OF EDUCATION

One of the greatest untapped sources for staff development is the available assistance and support services in the State Department of Education.

The mission of the State Department usually includes the following:

- offers opportunities to develop competence in the basic skills of communication, computations, and knowledge of basic facts concerning the environment, history, and society.
- provides opportunities to develop higher order thinking and problem-solving skills by means of adequate preparation in mathematics, science, the social sciences, and foreign languages and through appropriate and progressive use of technology.
- instills the ability and desire to continue learning throughout life.
- encourages knowledge and understanding of political society and democracy in order to foster active participation.

- motivates the creative potential through exposure to the fine arts and humanities.
- promotes a basic understanding of, and aids the development of, good health habits.
- creates opportunities for career exploration and awareness.

The Department of Education is an agency which provides leadership for education in the state while fulfilling regulatory services required by the state statutes. A conscious effort should be made to use the resources available. Utilizing the many areas of expertise and consultant services is advantageous in providing quality programs and services to a school district.

NETWORKING WITH OTHER SCHOOL DISTRICTS

Networking is a valuable means to enhance staff development services. The communication and sharing of programs can provide additional opportunities, knowledge, and resources. Purposes should be clearly identified along with timelines, agendas, and responsibilities. Therefore, meetings will have content and value to all those who commit time and effort to this process.

Suggestions for networking committee purposes would include:

- identifying contact persons in other school districts having responsibilities for staff development.
- sharing printed materials (e.g., catalog, policy statements, calendars, rationale, etc.).
- providing a cooperative venture in staff development through consultants and other current resources.
- communicating by meeting regularly, to cooperatively design courses, discuss concerns, announce offerings, workshops, and conferences.
- providing continuity for program implementation.
- consolidating practices, avoiding duplication of unrelated training fragments.

BUSINESS AND INDUSTRY

The rapidly changing world of high technology and career specialization presents a challenge to the existing educational structure. Ultimate change depends primarily upon effective working relationships with business and industry.

Business and education share the responsibility of preparing our youth for successful careers. The objective is to confront the limitations of traditional approaches to education and business, and explore new avenues of communication and understanding. Mutually beneficial projects for equal growth opportunities are essential in this endeavor. There are a variety of options available to strengthen the school-business alliance. They can be as varied as the identified need exists.

Activities may include guest speakers, tours, course offerings, instructional materials, sharing of facilities, exchange of personnel, student and staff training, honors banquets, promotional campaigns, and fairs. Implementation of these activities by school and business could evolve into an adopt-a-school partnership. This program allows for the professional growth of those who coordinate the program as well as the enrichment of personnel, students, and community members in a multitude of aspects. The key element would necessitate two representative coordinators—one from business and one from education. Specific projects and action steps can be identified using collaborative planning and involvement from selected participants. Increased awareness and communication on the part of both institutions will result. The vital source of enrichment in this alliance will bring a greater understanding into the world of work, thus addressing one of the primary goals of education.

PROFESSIONAL ORGANIZATIONS

Staff need to be aware of professional conferences and other organizational activities that can provide opportunities for new knowledge, and enhancement of previous knowledge and skills. Membership and active participations that address problems of the profession or service in which professionals are engaged is a recognized factor of professionalism. Staff must be encouraged to continue such relationships, in order to keep current through attendance to local state and national conferences for continuous professional learning.

POSTSECONDARY INVOLVEMENT

Institutions of higher learning represent a valuable resource for inservice and staff development workshops. These institutions have personnel who, if identified, can render valuable service on a variety of topics. It is suggested that staff development leadership think through the specifics of what is desired from the faculty of the institution of higher learning, and approach this person or persons with specific requests. The nature of the request will be open for discussion and compromise. However, the request should be specific; specificity will help the contributor to provide the services requested.

The specific contributions and involvement of faculty from colleges and universities might well include direct exchange of services, such as a college professor teaching in the public school, and the classroom teacher assuming responsibility for a college class. Serving as consultants for inquiry-based projects as well as observing within a classroom setting are other possibilities. The opportunities are many and varied. A better job of tapping these resources lies in the domain of the public school.

The above represent a sampling of the major agencies which can foster collaborative effort between the public schools and outside resource people and agencies. The concept of building relationships for success is sound and worthy of careful attention within staff development projects.

THE SYNERGISTIC EFFECT

As has been indicated previously, relationships for success involve bringing together those agencies and persons who can and will constructively contribute to the proposed project. The selection of personnel from the various agencies falls upon the shoulders of the director of staff development. The objective is to secure the right "mix" of people so that the overt objectives of the project will be carefully considered and hidden agendas will be at a minimum level.

All participants do not bring the same strengths to the meeting. Thus, the combination of people must represent a cross section of skills required for the task at hand. A carefully selected group representing a variety of agencies as represented in Figure 4 can result in a constructive project.

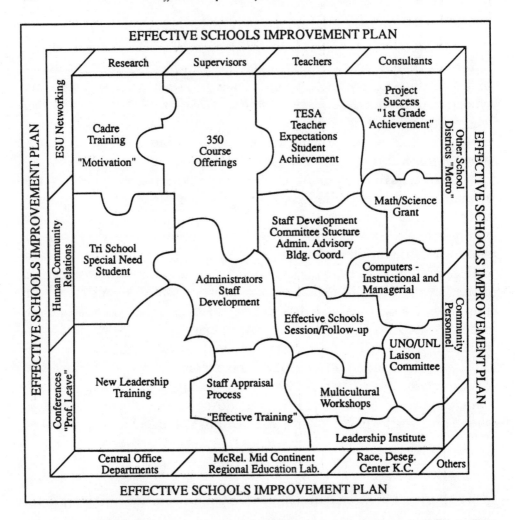

- The puzzle displays many of the interlocking pieces that comprise Staff Development Services. This model includes the parts which make staff operate effectively.

- The frame matting depicts the people services that provide the expertise, assistance, teaching, coaching and coordination of efforts.

- The title frame indicates the need for truly effective schools and the constant need to develop improvement plans.

Figure 4. Staff Development Services Model—"The Frame of Reality."

INFORMING THE PUBLIC

"P.R.," unfortunately, only too often is associated with a glitzy treatment of a situation or topic. Sound public relations involves informing one's constituency with the correct facts, utilizing those delivery systems which will reach the greatest number of people. As a generalization, schools have not devoted enough attention to publicizing their constructive achievements.

Achieving recognition and support for local accomplishments involves a multifacted approach. Based upon a project which has been carefully structured, developed by an interlocking of a network of concerned people, the challenge of informing the public is easier than a project which has not had careful thought and direction. If the vast majority of participants feel that "this is a good project," information dissemination becomes easier. The "bottom line" in public relations is the planning and execution of a sound project. Starting with quality, utilizing the channels of the press and word of mouth, and showing positive outcomes of the project, good "public relations" should follow. There is no substitute for quality. The knowledgeable director of staff development knows this and strives for quality in all undertakings.

REFERENCES

Bey, T. M. (April, 1986). Complete Procedural Record: Helping Beginning Teachers Set Professional Goals. *The Clearing House.*

Brandt, R. S. (1986). On Teachers Coaching Teachers: A Conversation with Bruce Joyce. *Educational Leadership,* Vol. 44, No. 5, pp. 12–17.

Bruce, J. and Weil, M. (1980). *Models of Teaching.* Englewood Cliffs, NJ: Prentice Hall, Second edition.

Cogan, M. (1973). *Clinical Supervision.* Boston: Houghton-Mifflin.

Johnson, D. and Johnson, R. (1984). *Circles of Learning.* Washington, DC: Association for Supervision and Curriculum Development.

McGreal, T. L. (1983). *Successful Teacher Evaluation.* Alexandria, VA: Association for Supervision and Curriculum Development.

CHAPTER 7

BENCHMARKS FOR SUCCESS OR FAILURE

S uccess, partial success, or failure of a given project or projects must be measured against a set of objectives. Staff development's major goal is to "stretch" the professional. The teacher must strive to scale new heights in his/her field of expertise. If growth and new horizons are indeed attainable, then a set of goals or objectives must serve as the benchmark for evaluation.

A set of attributes which can be utilized to measure increased teacher effectiveness might include the following:

- evidence of internalization of the project.
- internalization exemplified by a feeling of project "ownership."
- knowledge base broadened and utilized.
- examples of collaboration among teachers is evident.
- collegiality is prevalent.
- noted willingness to practice the new skill.
- use of positive reinforcement by leadership.
- project has been tried and interlocks with the total curricular program.
- provision has been made by leadership to provide for those materials, and conditions necessary to implement the project.
- appropriate information to board of education and community is provided.
- the process and the product are both important elements in measuring effectiveness.
- indicators of success are determined and used periodically.

A good summary of the challenges for the degree of success of a project are inherent in Figure 5.

The staff development instructional model is derived by literally stretching the knowledge base of the individual staff member. The center box in Figure 6 labeled "MUST KNOW," represents common learnings based on past experiences and preteaching preparation. The "SHOULD KNOW" box represents the direct assistance and knowledge provided by building

"STAFF DEVELOPMENT"

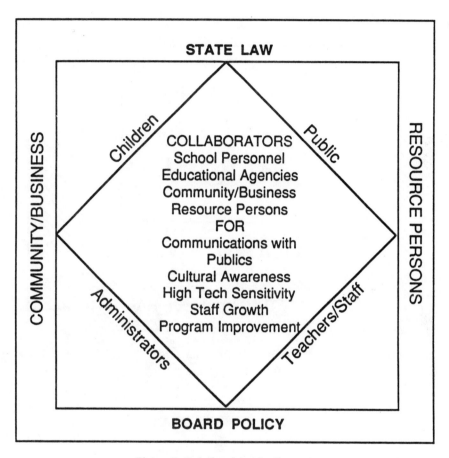

Figure 5. Relationships for Success.

leaders, immediate supervisors, support staff, peers, parents, lead teachers, and others. The "COULD KNOW" is what staff development training is all about. It represents both the cognitive and affective domain. The basic model was designed to help staff members become the best they can be. The body of knowledge in the "SHOULD KNOW" area also enhances, supports, and reinforces the staff member by helping to instill pride, confidence, and the intrinsic desire to bring about successful practices.

The components previously discussed are the general benchmarks utilized to measure progress. Further clarification may help provide specific directions for the professional.

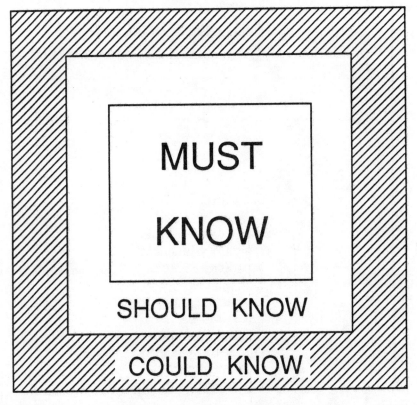

Figure 6. The Instructional Content. Adapted from Mills, H.R., Teaching and Training, A Handbook for Instructors, New York, 1977.

FACULTY FEEDBACK

Staff members using a new practice or process should first consider these questions:

- Do I have sufficient transfer skills and knowledge to utilize the new practice professionally with students?
- Am I prepared with specific sequential steps to present a developmental learning package?
- Is my classroom climate and organization conducive to this type of change?
- Have I gained enough confidence to effectively change my teaching style or embark on new unfamiliar content?
- Is the risk taking worth the time and effort it requires to make the necessary change?

- Will I give it a real try by using each step and evaluating only after having used it enough to qualify the results?
- Can I use it effectively as presented or with modification?
- Will it become an internalized part of my instruction?

Securing quality feedback is often difficult since each staff member is usually coming from a different place in practice. Skill acquisition, too, is never consistent. A great deal depends on the modeling process used in training and the intensity, practice, and sustained support provided for the staff members.

Surveys, small group discussions, monitoring, and oral questioning will often help one evaluate the effectiveness of a new program. Students' comments and classroom observations often will provide further insight and needed evidence. We must remember to use time as the measuring barometer for reliable feedback. Staff should have used the practice or process sufficiently to provide a proper measurement. Four to six weeks is sufficient for a strand, concept, or segment to become a part of the students' learning content.

Supervisors, department chairpersons, parents, and students are excellent evaluators as long as they have knowledge of the content and objective. Research-supported activities will often gain credibility, if the research as well as the training guides are reviewed often to help clarify and analyze procedures. It is also possible that collegial discussion groups formed for the purpose of sharing, questioning and modifying procedures will become a motivating factor. It is important to respect the teacher's prerogative to abandon the practice if it appears too stressful and inhibits learning.

STUDENT PERFORMANCE AND PRODUCTIVITY

Staff developers should keep the agenda targeted upon student performance. The project must be committed to the idea of student success in school. Much national attention by the media has been focused upon tests, the testing process, and lack of achievement by children in American schools. The focus tends to be upon securing high test scores by all children. In such a frame of reference test results are looked upon as the final indication of academic "victory," "rigor," and "conquering" of ignorance. The above is the alleged ultimate goal in education.

Yet, there are many other uses of teacher-made tests besides aiming for a perfect score. Teachers utilize pretests to learn the level of understanding and knowledge before teaching new material. Tests are used to provide feedback on the student learning progress during a given unit. Tests are used to determine improvements in achievement. Tests can be used to assist in making instructional revisions. These represent a sampling of the various uses of tests and test scores. The teacher's tests used as diagnostic instruments are perhaps the dimension least understood by the lay public.

Writing a set of clear comprehensible objectives, for whatever the educational project may be, is standard procedure. For example, when developing a new curricular program, the objectives for the curriculum and the test items must be compatible. The two must mesh. Let us discover what we know, where the knowledge voids are located, and then teach for mastery—teach well what we test and in this way avoid continual remediation.

Interpreting test scores and teaching accordingly can bring about desired results. The practice of disaggregating the scores to determine the specific needs of individual children is an effective practice to further individualize instruction.

Other evidences of student performance and productivity include the degree of student involvement in class discussion and activity, accompanied by feelings of student pride, self-confidence, and being a supportive member of the group. These are vital factors to student growth and development.

EXTERNAL ASSESSMENT

Schools, in essence, do belong to society. Therefore, they must go beyond themselves to evaluate, assess or measure success, growth, or direction. Regardless of the quality, size, or effectiveness of a school district, external assessment is essential to continued growth of excellence.

Educators must continually look for answers, measure outcomes, and expand their knowledge to do an even better job as they plan for the future. More and more is expected of the schools of today, thus challenging staff developers to provide the training and expertise to make it happen. External assistance can stimulate the need for human and organizational improvements that will meet the need of an ever-changing society.

One must enter the external self-study process with renewed interest and optimism, that constitutes a constructive critical look at what is being recommended can enhance a positive and substantive change for the district. There are many resources available to substantiate change. A wealth of research and development has been made available to educators that describes practical steps, follow-up procedures, and training to successfully implement programs for the classrooms of today.

Rapid and complex changes in education reform have been thrust upon school districts. This has forced schools to seek assistance externally. Post-secondary institutions, state departments of education, national accrediting associations, professional organizations, regional laboratories, business, and industry have played important roles in this endeavor. The staff development challenge lies with the use of training models that address the need to help staff members who have been prepared to work in a simpler, more traditional setting that no longer exists. Long-range staff development should be able to utilize effectively the external recommendations. If staff development is a key component, staff need to be active committee members of the self-study and evaluation groups, write the reports, and be engaged in the follow-up. Parents and community members, too, serve on the visiting team, thus allowing for another dimension to ownership and implementation.

REPORTING TO THE BOARD/SUPERINTENDENT

Staff developers must remain close to all departments and divisions when formulating the district's long-range staff development plans, since the content area is concerned primarily with curriculum instruction, staff and student personnel, and community relations. Staff development is the catalyst to make things happen. Course content is governed by the stated district goals, recommendations of various external assessment, school improvement planning, expressed staff needs, and current research trends.

Working closely with the superintendent to accomplish the district's stated goals should constitute the basic program structure. How one works in this framework can be as creative and innovative as the targeted audiences will allow. It is important that the superintendent be kept informed regarding workshop activities, evaluations, student outcomes, staff participation, school success or failures, grant possibilities, and all other facets within the realm of training.

Garnering support from the board of education comes from current knowledge and accurate information regarding the staff development programs. Staff developers should maintain regular reporting schedules of informative projects or activities to the board committees. This will help with the finances and policy to support the varied needs of training. The board of education, too, must see the need, new rationale, and the desired outcomes.

Preparing to present to the board is an important endeavor which requires careful planning summarized in a concise, but informative, paper. It should be organized in a manner so it can be understood without explanation, approved by the superintendent, and sent to the board members' homes prior to the meeting. The content of the report should follow this outline:

- philosophical overview.
- program objectives.
- participants (who was involved, schools, grade level, or curriculum area).
- costs and utilization of resources.
- desired outcomes (measurement criteria).
- long-range plans.
- on-site participants may share projects and application of training concepts.

THE PUBLIC RELATIONS DIMENSION

Schools belong to the people; thus, they have a legal and moral right to know what transpires within the institution. Good public relations, "P.R.," conveys an understanding of the goals, objectives, achievements, and frustrations of the organization.

Each child who goes home daily with a positive message of a constructive experience can represent a far better public relations device than a story written by a principal or a representative from the press. In brief, good "P.R." is composed of many approaches and various techniques. Staff development is an important function deserving a more positive public image. The fact is overlooked that teachers, perhaps to a greater degree than many professions, do indeed have a built in mechanism for keeping current, namely the staff development process. Activities such as workshops, seminars, and professional meetings tend not to be grist for newspaper articles or TV coverage. However, these activities do indeed represent a significant investment of time and professional effort, and should come to the attention of parents and the general public. The media must come to recognize that staff development projects are indeed newsworthy, and do represent high profile activity to communicate the idea that teachers are committed to continued up-dating and learning. The teaching profession is making a genuine effort to keep on "the cutting edge."

Public relations for staff development can be fostered through the following:

- Use the school newsletter to relate the objectives of staff training segments and expected outcomes.
- Secure a press conference or interview with the visiting staff development consultant, focusing on major community concerns.
- Invite an adopt-a-school business or agency representative to participate.
- Utilize university and other postsecondary institutions to serve as facilitators or moderators.
- Publicize the external team recommendations which promote training needs.
- Use parent and other school-community meetings to inform the public about the new training techniques.
- Utilize staff in "telling their story" of the benefits of the program and use of the new knowledge.
- Recognize that children are the best conveyers of the school message; get them informed and involved in the process.
- Publicly recognize staff efforts, commitment and achievement. Demonstrate with the students the effects of the program.
- Avoid professional terminology of the educator when communicating with the public.
- Include achievements as well as disappointments.
- Go beyond written communication and utilize the electronic media to reach various facets of the community.
- Maintain quality control of the material being disseminated.
- Maintain an on-going flow of information. Continually market the program benefits to gain support and recognition.

INTERRELATIONSHIPS WITH
THE TOTAL SCHOOL PROGRAM

Making sure that the new staff development project has a place in the total learning environment of the school is an important issue—one that must be given careful and thoughtful consideration. Teachers and administrators do not need an additional project or program. What they do need is more helpful, constructive ways to reach students by utilizing theory, practice, and application in practical ways. Education is an intimate, human, participatory, active, and labor intensive business. One activity reinforces another—training and knowledge are an integral part of that process.

It is people helping people, more art than science and more personal than technical (Meade, 1986). The teacher, not the curriculum, is the key element in achieving results. We must be careful not to provide training that is in small isolated segments where staff members do not see interrelationships and linkages to other teaching learning techniques. The goal is that the learning activity achieves the objective in the simplest way possible, is comfortable for participants, consistent with the learner's expectations, and contains required specialized skills and will yield new learnings.

REFERENCES

Hall, C. E. and Loucks. (September, 1978). S. F. Teacher Concerns as a Basis for Facilitating and Personalizing Staff Development. *Teachers College Record*, Vol. 80, No. 1, pp. 36–53.

Mangiere, J. H. and Kemper, R. E. (1983). Administrators: The Key to Successful In-service Programs. *NASSP Bulletin*, Vol. 67, No. 461, pp. 26–31.

Meade, L. T. (1986). Chart of Change. *Childrens Literature in Education*. Albany, NY: Agathon Press.

Ward, B. A. and Tkinoff, W. J. (1982). Collaborative Research: Implications of Research & Practice. Washington, DC: National Institute of Education.

Wood, F. H. and Thompson, S. R. (1980). Guidelines for Better Staff Development. *Educational Leadership*, Vol. 37, pp. 374–378.

CHAPTER 8

PUTTING IT ALL TOGETHER

The purpose of this chapter is to provide a guideline or a map for the novice staff development coordinator who may be experiencing her/his first major project. Also, the sequential listing of events can serve as a check list for the seasoned coordinator who understands the importance of "covering all bases" in the preparation for the delivery of a staff development project.

The major areas identified represent the seven chapter headings of the publication. These seven topical areas concern:

- societal demands and staff development.
- current trends in staff development.
- organizational design for staff development.
- planning, delivery of staff development.
- implementation: key element.
- relationships for success.
- benchmarks for success or failure.

PROCEDURE

In reviewing the items listed under each of the topics, the coordinator by responding with a "yes" or "no," contains a systematic run-down of vital items needing attention in any staff development project. It is obvious that settings and projects vary from school system to school system. Yet, there is a set of constants in every project which needs consideration. It is to this objective that the writers have directed this chapter.

THE MASTER CHECKLIST

PROGRAMMATIC-CATEGORIES	HAVE I/WE CONSIDERED:	YES	NO
SOCIETAL DEMANDS	the changing student population?		
"The school serves as a mirror	the expanded curricular demands?		
reflecting the desires of the	developing technology?		
community."	the influence of pressure groups?		
	complexity of society?		
	staff needs/competencies in curriculum/ instructional strategies?		

	HAVE I/WE CONSIDERED?		
CURRENT TRENDS	identifying the elements that constitute		
"Change is implicit in considera-	quality staff development?		
tion of current trends."	the available resources?		
	a staff development model or plan?		
	the uniqueness of the adult learner?		
	selecting appropriate help?		
	• consultants?		
	• in-house expertise?		
	• training of trainers?		
	• peer coaches?		
	• building leadership?		
	translation to an operational model?		

	HAVE I/WE CONSIDERED?		
ORGANIZATIONAL DESIGN	a philosophy in keeping with district		
"Organizational design should	goals?		
determine program impact upon	the mission and goals of the project?		
students through improvement of	a policy statement to accommodate staff		
human resources."	development activities?		
	the function of all segments?		
	• superintendent?		
	• staff		
	• office		
	• committee		
	• buildings		
	• support groups		

	HAVE I/WE CONSIDERED?		
PLANNING AND DELIVERY OF STAFF DEVELOPMENT			
"Thorough planning of program	adequate budget to cover stated program?		
shapes the format for delivery of	the use of a needs assessment?		
staff development activities."	the timing and scheduling of events?		
	the appropriateness of format and content?		
	staff involvement in the initial planning?		

PROGRAMMATIC-CATEGORIES	HAVE I/WE CONSIDERED:	YES	NO
	program identification as related to other areas?	___	___
	a specific delivery of services to support the program?	___	___
	the program in sequential steps to accomodate transfer of knowledge?	___	___
	provisions made for monitoring all steps of the program?	___	___
	soundness of the program?	___	___
	project's interlocking with the established ongoing curriculum?	___	___
	the scheduling of activities and events in realistic terms of time frames?	___	___
	the organizational design as it relates to the practitioner?	___	___

IMPLEMENTATION:
KEY ELEMENTS
(IS THE PROGRAM WORKING?)
"Effective implementation cements the promise for achieving desired outcomes."

	HAVE I/WE CONSIDERED:	YES	NO
	the participants' attainment of knowledge and skills?	___	___
	student performance?	___	___
	long-range plans?	___	___
	sustaining effort and revisiting the research?	___	___
	evidence of real change?	___	___
	support assistance?	___	___
	team effort?	___	___
	acceptance of change?	___	___
	awarding of credit and reinforcing staff?	___	___
	transformation stages indicating higher levels of competence?	___	___

RELATIONSHIPS FOR SUCCESS
"Collaborative efforts are the essence of success."

	HAVE I/WE CONSIDERED?	YES	NO
	identifying representative collaborators?	___	___
	inviting and involving representative groups?	___	___
	involving school personnel?	___	___
	networking with educational agencies?	___	___
	collaborating with business/industry?	___	___
	using resource consultants?	___	___
	student involvement?	___	___
	utilizing the research component?	___	___

BENCHMARKS FOR
SUCCESS/FAILURE

"Involvement of people will
provide the means to successful
endeavors."

HAVE I/WE CONSIDERED?

measuring for success/failure? ___ ___

assessing the accomplishments against
the stated objective? ___ ___

indicators of staff productivity? ___ ___

student performance? ___ ___

provision for administration and
board support? ___ ___

relating the project outcomes to
the public? ___ ___

a marketing plan? ___ ___

inter-relationships with other school
programs? ___ ___

CHAPTER 9

INCORPORATING THE ESSENTIAL PRACTICES: MODELS FOR THE PRACTITIONER

Time is of the essence for the staff developer. It is one of the most labor-intensified assignments. Therefore, the practitioner is constantly in need or a ready-made hands-on sampling of modes, plans, agendas, projects, and evaluations, to be studied and utilized prior to launching a project. The following represent a sampling of models which can be instrumental for the implementation of a well-designed staff development program. School districts should establish a common base in the form of specific goals, objectives, and procedures which provide the structure for program development and communication in the staff development process.

DISTRICT GOALS/SUPERINTENDENT OBJECTIVES

District goals and the superintendent's objectives are the basic guidelines for any staff development program. These criteria provide the "umbrella" for all staff development activities.

MODEL 1
GOALS FOR THE SCHOOL DISTRICT

Introduction

The Superintendent of Schools named a steering committee to explore the possibility of examining the school district's commitment to public education through a study of its educational goals. As a result, the committee recommended that a cooperative, systematic study be pursued to determine methods to be used to review and restructure the existing purposes of the school system in light of current societal trends.

Process

Through the series of actions described below, the recommended goals were devised.

- Planning sessions were scheduled to determine methods to obtain suggestions for goals.
- Consultants were employed to assist in planning, implementing, and training sessions.
- Two thousand seven hundred (2,700) staff participated in a district-wide goal-setting workshop.
- Suggested goals were categorized and synthesized by a task force.
- The goal-setting process was presented to the Planning Committee of the Board of Education.
- Proposed goals were submitted to the schools and divisions for staff and community input.
- Surveys were received from the respective schools and divisions for further review and analysis.
- All goals that were rated extremely desirable or very desirable by at least 85 percent of the respondents were used to formulate the general goal statements. Goals that were rated extremely desirable or very desirable by at least 75 percent were also used to formulate subgoal statements.
- A set of ten goals was reviewed by the leadership team (i.e., 270 administrators) and the Citizens Advisory Committee.

STATEMENT OF PHILOSOPHY

The Board of Education of the School District is responsible for meeting the challenge of providing a comprehensive educational program in an atmosphere that is open, concerned, and responsive to the needs of students and the community. To this end, the Board of Education establishes policies that are translated into practices and procedures by the Superintendent and staff to maintain and improve the quality of teaching and learning. The following statements express the philosophy that guided the school district in the formation of its goals and objectives:

We Believe

All students have an inherent right to an education that will enable them to reach their highest possible intellectual, social, physical, and ethical development.

Education must concentrate on the complete development of students as individuals and as citizens.

Quality education programs and a committed staff provide learners with the knowledge and skills necessary for full participation in our changing society.

The responsibility of education in a democracy is to make it possible for all citizens to understand themselves and the world about them, so that they can live effectively in the world of expanding experiences and constant change.

Education requires systematic and sustained effort by students, staff, parents, and community.

Education is a life-long process.

GOALS

The following goals provide the context for educational planning.

For the Learner

1. Maintain and improve academic achievement.
2. Develop aesthetic appreciation and ability.
3. Understand the free enterprise system and the meaning of economic self-sufficiency.
4. Understand the rights and responsibilities of citizenship.
5. Acquire the insights, knowledge, and skills necessary for the development of physical and mental health.

For the Staff

6. Promote excellence in student achievement by maintaining high standards of professionalism, preparation, and performance.
7. Provide educational programs designed to promote the attainment of knowledge, competencies, and skills by students.

For the School System and Community

8. Insure access and equity for students in their pursuit of educational opportunities in a pluralistic society.
9. Provide adequate financial support and professional opportunities for staff.
10. Build public confidence and attain economic resources to accomplish the goals of the school system.

MODEL II
PROPOSED BUDGET PARAMETERS OF SCHOOL DISTRICT

The budget will provide for:

- A commitment to Board of Education goals and priorities.
- Student educational experiences which reach beyond fundamental skills through productive programs which meet the unique needs of our student body.
- Continued commitment to the desegregation plan.
- Comprehensive multicultural educational experiences and cultural-human awareness opportunities for students, staff, and parents throughout the district.
- Continued recruitment, selection, and employment of the best available personnel.
- Efficient and productive appraisal of all employees.
- Effective annual analysis and evaluation of programs and services.
- Comprehensive special education services designed to meet the needs of handicapped students in compliance with Rule 51 and P.L. 94-142.
- Continued educational, personal, and career counseling services for students.
- Continuation of computer-assisted instruction.
- Reasonable salary and fringe benefit adjustments.
- Current student-teacher and class size rations.
- Effective custodial, maintenance, transportation, and food service programs which insure a safe, healthy, and appropriate educational environment for students.
- Beginning implementation phase of facility needs assessment.
- *Staff development programs designed to promote professional growth and development.*

- A communications program which reaches all forms of media and the various sectors of the community.
- Continued improvement of management capabilities through the use of technology.
- Continuation of cooperative efforts with parents, business, industry, and other community organizations to enhance educational opportunities for students.
- Continued maintenance of support services necessary to insure the availability of programs and materials for all students enrolled in the public schools.

DISTRICT-WIDE PROGRAMS/
VIA THE STAFF DEVELOPMENT COORDINATOR

District-wide programs are those designed to serve the identified common concerns of the district and complement the stated district goals and objectives of the Superintendent.

MODEL III
PROJECT SUCCESS

Project Success was initiated to comply with the schools mission statement "that all students have an inherent right to an education that will enable them to reach their highest possible intellectual, social, physical, and ethical development."

The Superintendent requested that staff explore possibilities to raise first grade achievement in targeted areas. Representative staff were invited to a planning session where need, focus, and appropriate activities were determined. A support team was identified and a time segment framed.

Purpose

- Provide effective instructional training
- Raise first-grade student achievement in the primary grade level centers and other target schools
- Assist staff in instructional strategies, planning, and implementation
- Organize a support segment for first grade teachers

Involvement

The following public and nonpublic schools met regularly during the school year to work with action plans:

Activities/Projects

Work Sessions:

August

Topics addressed:

- Defining a purpose/need
- Looking at expectations of child/teacher
- Clarifying outcomes
- Learning the essentials of instructional planning
- Knowing classroom management techniques
- Writing action plans

January (3:45 to 7:00 p.m.)

Topics addressed:

- Refining and assessing action plans
- Enhancing self-motivation skills
- Exploring instructional testing strategies
- Planning for future sessions

February (3:45 to 7:00 p.m.)

Topics addressed:

- Writing activities for identified objectives
- Learning test terminology and administrative strategies
- Exploring problem solving activities appropriate for grade one

June

Topics addressed:

- Reviewing goals and achievements, including test analysis
- Identifying new directions the project should take during the school year
- Developing personal and building level action plans
- Defining a calendar of events for the projects
- Identifying specific outcomes for planning of teaching techniques

Outcomes

Table 1 shows the percentage of first grade students who scored above the 50th percentile rank on each of the subtests of the *California Achievement Tests* administered in the spring of 1986 and 1987. Large gains were made by the students in Project Success schools. The lowest gain was in the Language Expression subtest and the highest in Reading Comprehension where 56 percent of the students scored above the 50th percentile rank. The most dramatic accomplishments were made by students in the Mathematics subtests where approximately 70 percent and 62 percent of the students scored above the 50th percentile rank in the Computation and Concepts/Applications subtests respectively.

Table 2 shows the percentage of students who scored in each percentile rank quarter. A smaller percentage of students scored in the lowest quarter in 1987 and a larger percentage scored in the highest quarter in 1987.

Table 1.
Project Success
California Achievement Test Results
Percent of Students Scoring Above 50th Percentile Rank
Year 1 Compared to Year 2

	Percent		
Subtest	*Year 2*	*Year 1*	*Change*
Vocabulary	53.9	27.4	+26.5
Comprehension	56.0	26.4	+29.6
Expression	38.8	20.7	+18.1
Computation	71.2	45.6	+25.6
Concepts & Applications	61.8	42.2	+19.6

Table 2.
Project Success—Grade 1
California Achievement Test Results
Percent of Students Scoring in Percentile Rank Quarter
Year 1 Compared to Year 2

Subtest	Year 2	Year 1	Year 2	Year 1	Year 2	Year 1	Year 2	Year 1
Vocabulary	18.7	44.8	27.5	27.8	26.2	16.3	27.7	11.1
Comprehension	23.5	54.8	20.5	18.8	31.9	16.3	24.1	10.1
Expression	23.3	51.6	37.8	27.7	21.2	12.4	17.6	8.3
Computation	13.1	29.3	15.8	25.1	33.7	25.5	37.5	20.1
Concepts & Applications	16.6	33.7	21.6	24.1	24.7	23.7	37.1	18.5

Future Plans

Use the McRel vocabulary program that identifies 7300 concepts found at the elementary school level and organizes them into 61 instructional clusters. This is designed to help staff to provide direct instruction in those concepts necessary to improve reading and overall performance.

Prepared by: Approved by:
Staff Development Services   Superintendent of Schools

MODEL IV
INSERVICE TRAINING FOR
ELEMENTARY TEACHERS IN THE PHYSICAL SCIENCES

In response to your stated interest and need . . .

WHAT: An inservice designed specifically for elementary teachers in the areas of chemistry, physical and earth science is offered.

WHERE: Junior High—Room #204

WHO: Taught by University—Science Education Professor

WHEN: Time—3:45 to 5:30 p.m.

Dates—Wednesdays—February, March, April

Each participant will receive a stipend for each session attended, as well as Professional Growth. In exchange for this quality, inservice training and stipend, participants will be expected to serve as a resource person for their building and district. Participants will provide information in methodology and demonstrations in content areas to staff through inservice programs at their building or district level.

If interested, please complete the registration blank provided below and send to:

Staff Development Services
PLEASE RETURN THIS FORM ON OR BEFORE JANUARY 31

NAME _____
GRADE LEVEL TAUGHT _____
SCHOOL DISTRICT _____
BUILDING _____
ADDRESS _____
PHONE _____
PRINCIPAL'S SIGNATURE _____

NOTE: Your application will be reviewed and, if selected, you will be notified.

INDIVIDUAL SCHOOL REQUESTS

Individual school activities may be formulated by using the staff to develop plans. The staff development coordinator may facilitate the training session by assisting with planning, objectives, organizational format, finances, consultant services, agenda, evaluation and follow-up procedures.

Below are samples showing this practice:

MODEL V
ALTERNATIVE CENTER INSERVICE

Goals: To develop effective, efficient interaction among team members. (Day 01)
To identify methods of meeting special learning needs of behaviorally impaired students. (Day 02).
To increase effective instructional time through classroom management techniques. (Day 02)
To understand the message behind the behavior. (Day 02)

Day 01 August

8:15	Rolls and Coffee	Teacher
8:30	Welcome	
	Introduction	
	Background of Program	
8:45	Remarks	Principal
9:00	Working Effectively Within a Team	Consultant
10:15	Break	
10:30	Continue—Working Effectively Within a Team	Consultant
12:00	Lunch (On Your Own)	
1:00	You As Team Member	Consultant
2:00	Break	
2:15	Continue—You As Team Member	Consultant
3:30	Dismiss	

Day 02 August

8:15	Rolls and Coffee	
8:30	Mastery Learning	Supervisor
10:15	Break	
10:30	Putting Mastery Into Practice	Teacher
11:30	Lunch (On Your Own)	
12:30	Adlerian Theory	University Professor
1:45	Break	
2:00	Goals of Misbehavior	University Professor
3:30	Dismiss	

MODEL VI
IMPROVING INSTRUCTIONAL SKILLS

AGENDA

4:00–5:15	Instructional Strategies
	• Mapping
	• Unison Reading
	• Visualization
5:15–5:50	Supper Break

5:50–6:15	Language Experience Approach to Instruction
6:15–7:00	Student Activity Cards Addressing Outcomes
	• Math cards designed last season
	• Developing new cards

OBJECTIVES

Participants will:

- Improve instructional skills in mapping, unison reading and visualization.
- Review the use of the Language Experience approach to instruction.
- Develop student activity cards to address outcomes.

Expected Outcomes of the Workshop

As a result of the workshop, participants will do the following:

1. Review project goals and achievements including test analysis.
2. Identify new directions the project should take during the 1987–88 school year.
3. Develop personal or building level action plans for the year.
4. Define a calendar of events for the project for next year.
5. Identify specific outcomes for planning of teaching techniques.

MODEL VII
ACTION PLAN

1. List the three most important learning needs that should be met in your school (or classroom) to raise first grade test scores to the next quartile. (Write about what changes you would like to see in the skill and knowledge of the children, not the changes in school organization.)

    1. _____
    2. _____
    3. _____

2. Write three goal statements to show what your school should accomplish this year to answer the needs listed above.

    1. _____
    2. _____
    3. _____

3. For each goal, tell how you will be able to prove the goal has been met.

GOAL 1

_____

_____

_____

GOAL 2

_____

_____

_____

GOAL 3

_____

_____

_____

4. For each goal write 3–5 steps you plan to take in your school or classroom to reach the goal. List the action, who will do it, and when it will be finished.

GOAL 1

ACTION	WHO	WHEN
_____	_____	_____
_____	_____	_____
_____	_____	_____

LEADERSHIP INSERVICE

Leadership inservice is designed with the close assistance of an advisory team. Leadership provides direction, vision for the future and pragmatic solutions of the daily concerns and problems of the organization. This training should center upon the needs of practicing administrators, newly appointed leaders and those persons aspiring to the role of leader. As effort is focused upon this three-dimensional program, thus, a bank of talent is developed for the school system.

MODEL VIII
LEADERSHIP DEVELOPMENT INSTITUTE

The past 35 years, an annual leadership seminar has been conducted for selected staff members showing an interest in the district's administrative functions. This activity has proven beneficial since it was informative and often provided a talent pool used in selecting staff for administrative positions. In light of changing times and the never-ending need and demand for quality personnel to perform leadership tasks, a more comprehensive program structure was designed for training interested applicants. The institute model provides an in-depth approach with emphasis upon learning experiences which focus on the development of specific leadership and administrative skills. The institute spans a two-year cycle wherein the applicant will be involved in a process of selection beginning with a nomination and a formal application from the nominee. A screening process names the initial candidates after which interviews for final selection are conducted. A four-day workshop scheduled during the Spring Recess introduces the institute.

Special staff development courses will be offered to acquaint the participants with the identified competencies and skills. University courses, counseling, and postassessment activities are important components of the program.

Purposes:

To offer a leadership institute providing participants the opportunity to acquire an understanding, an appreciation and sensitivity to the role and function of administration.

To develop a reservoir of talent which may be used in making future leadership assignment decisions.

Objectives:

1. Increase awareness of the responsibility of administrative functions in the school district.
2. Gain an appreciation for and understanding of the school district.
3. Learn more about oneself by developing an individual training plan.

4. Provide professional growth opportunity.
5. Provide a forum for mutual acquaintance between participants and administration.

The Following Skills/Competencies Will Be Emphasized:

Organizing for Effective Administration
Resources and Logistical Management
Supervision and Evaluation
Effective Communication
Interpersonal Relationships
Planning, Organizing and Controlling
Decision-Making
Program Implications
Group Facilitation
Personal and Professional Growth
Instructional Leadership
Performance and Expectations
Other

PROGRAM FORMAT AND TIMELINE

YEAR 1

January	Presentation of Program to Elementary Principals
	Presentation of Program to Junior High Principals
	Presentation of Program to Senior High Principals
	Announcement by Letter (Admin/Supvrs)
	News Bulletin
February	Reminder at regular meeting of Administrators/ Supervisors
	Nominations Due
	Applications from Nominees Due
March	Screening Committee Process
	Saturday Interviews Conducted by Teams
	Screening Committee Selection of Participants
	Contact Presenters and Design Program Booklet
	Notification to Participants (Approx. 26)
	Institute Sessions—8:00–4:00 (Spring Break)
April through June	Course Selection and Training
	(a) Staff Development course offerings which address competencies

(b) University classes (depending upon certification and other needs)

(c) Committee involvement and work areas assigned

February through March

Postassessment (accompanied by written record for Personnel File)

MODEL IX
AGENDA
NEW APPRAISAL PROCESS WORKSHOP

Science Center

8:00 a.m.	Overview	Principal C Science Center
8:15	Performance Goals	Principal School X
8:40	Observations	Principal Z Junior High School and Principal A School
9:15	**BREAK**	
9:40	Planning/Teaching Materials	Principal D School
10:00	Rap Session/Idea Exchange Elementary	*Group Leaders:* Principal Science Center
	Secondary	Principal X High School

OBJECTIVES

To provide a better understanding of the New Staff Appraisal Process by:

- Clarifying the process as stated in the guide.
- Providing further information on the various segments of the process.
- Providing a forum for questions, discussions and answers.
- Sharing ideas, successes and problems.

NEW APPRAISAL PROCESS WORKSHOP EVALUATION
Science Center

	Yes	*No*
1. Do you have a better understanding of the various segments contained in the new appraisal process?	____	____
2. Are performance goals clear to you?	____	____
3. Do you feel more knowledgeable about the formal and informal observations?	____	____
4. Was the teaching/planning presentation helpful to you?	____	____
5. Did the rap session and idea exchange clear up some of your concerns?	____	____

What else do we need to do to help you implement the program?

_____

Other Comments:

OPENING SCHOOL ACTIVITIES

Launching a new school year requires genuine skill. The staff needs information relative to changes which have taken place over the summer and new developments anticipated during the upcoming year. The opening activities must be brief, specific, and directed to the objective of allowing time for the teacher to work in the classroom. "Setting up the Classroom" is the cornerstone of the opening school activities.

Below are samples of this process:

MODEL X
PRESCHOOL CONFERENCE FOR NEW STAFF

Thursday, August

HIGH SCHOOL

9:00	Coffee	Cafeteria
9:45	General Orientation	Auditorium
11:15	Professional Organizations and Activities	Auditorium
11:45	Professional Organization Luncheon	Cafeteria
1:30–4:00	Meetings with principals in assigned buildings	

Friday

PRIMARY TEACHERS—A SCHOOL

		Starting the Year Right
8:30–11:30	Room 5	Kindergarten
	Room 1	Grade 1
	Room 28	Grade 2
	Room 23	Grade 3

INTERMEDIATE TEACHERS—B SCHOOL

		Starting the Year Right
8:30–11:30	Room 9	Grade 4
	Room 7	Grade 5
	Room 18	Grade 6

Meet Your Supervisor: Questions and Answers

Room 18	Teacher
Room 9	Supervisor
Room 7	Lead Teacher
Room 6	Teacher

SECONDARY TEACHERS—HIGH SCHOOL

8:30–11:30

Room 327	Art	Room 213	JROTC
Room 331	Business Education	Library	Librarians
Room 308	Core	Room 201	Mathematics
Room 203	Driver Education	Room 337	Music
Room 341	English	Room 205	Physical Education
Room 315	Foreign Language	Room 323	Science
Room 336	Homemaking	Room 207	Social Studies
Room 232	Industrial Education	Room 208	Special Education

MODEL XI
OVERVIEW OF THE FALL CONFERENCE

Monday, August

8:30–11:30 a.m.	Teachers report to their assigned buildings
1:30–4:00 p.m.	Traveling Art Teachers report to Z School
	Traveling Music Teachers report to Lunchroom, District Office
	Traveling Physical Education Teachers report to C school

Elementary School
Elementary Nurses report to South Annex
Speech Therapists report to South Annex

Tuesday, August

8:30 a.m.   Opening General Session
                      City Auditorium

1:30–4:00 p.m.   Curriculum Meetings
                      Primary Teachers—Junior High School
                      Intermediate Teachers—Junior High School
                      Special Education—High School
                      Secondary Teachers—High School
                                      —Junior High School
                      Physical Education Teachers—
                        C Elementary School

Wednesday, August

8:30–11:30 a.m.   "Caring Is Basic"—High School
1:30–4:00 p.m.   Staff of buildings listed
8:30–11:30 a.m.   Staff report to their assigned buildings
1:30–4:00 p.m.

Thursday, August

                      Staff report to assigned building

Friday, August

8:30–11:30 a.m.   Curriculum Meetings
                      Primary Teachers—Junior High School
                      Intermediate Teachers—Junior High School
                      Special Education Teachers—High School
                      Secondary Teachers—High School
                                      —Junior High School
                      Physical Education Teachers—
                        D Elementary School
1:30–4:00 p.m.   Teachers report to their assigned buildings

MODEL XII
SCHOOL COUNSELOR—COMMUNITY CONFERENCE

Theme: "They All Have a Place"

8:00	Registration—Rolls and Coffee	
8:15	Introduction	Conference Chairman Rotary Club
8:20	History and Purpose of the School Counselor-Community Conference	Board Member
8:30	Education for Tomorrow's World Basic Attitudes	Professor Department of Secondary Education
	Preventive and corrective Programs	Director Department of Vocational and Adult Education
9:15	Coffee Break	
9:45	Discussion Groups—I have this idea; I have this question	
10:45	Sharing Ideas and Questions	
11:30	Summary Statement	Director of Guidance

MODEL XIII
STAFF DEVELOPMENT   # _____
PROPOSAL FOR INSERVICE OFFERINGS

Name of offering: _____

Objective or Purpose: _____

Description of offering: _____

Category (e.g., Business, Science, etc.) _____

Instructor(s): _____ Position: _____

Time: (clock hours) _____ Day(s) of week: _____

Dates (e.g., 10/3, 10/12, 11/12, 11/15): _____

Location: Building _____ Room No. _____

Maximum number of hours required to complete the activity: _____

Eligible participants: _____

Recommended minimum enrollment: _____ Maximum enrollment: _____

To your knowledge, has this activity been offered before? Yes ____ No ____

If yes, indicate last year offered: ____

Was it completed? Yes _____ No _____

Mark the group(s) involved in the planning and presenting of the offering.

_____ Public School Staff   _____ Post-Secondary

_____ Business and Industry   _____ State Dept. of Education

_____ Professional   _____ Community Agencies/

Organizations   Publics

_____ Other Districts   _____ Other Associations

_____ Date _____

  Signature of Person Responsible

_____ Date _____

 Assistant Superintendent/Director Approval

Date of Committee Review _____ Approved: ___ Yes ___ No

Date Approved by Professional Growth Committee _____ For _____
                # of points

White copy, Yellow copy: Staff Development Office   Pink copy: Your files

COURSE GUIDE VIA STAFF PROPOSALS

A current course guide for all staff, both certified and classified, is a practical means to provide communication of training opportunities. The guide is composed of offerings utilizing the approved proposal requests submitted by staff. This then serves as a summarized listing for participation through registration. Professional growth points can be assigned to each professional offering.

Below are sample forms of this procedure:

Course Guides: A Sampling

STUDENT TRANSPORTATION 022-024

#22 — *Van Driver Workshop*   PGP—0

  Workshop divided into two, 40-minute sessions, each session consisting of a panel presentation and small group discussion. Workshop covers needs of students with various handicaps and discusses ways to maintain positive relationships.

  Classification: Other Approved Activity

  Instructor: Human-Community Relations/Transportation

  Eligible Participants: Van & Bus Drivers and Aides

Location: Junior High School
Time: 8:30–11:30 a.m.
Dates: To be scheduled week before school starts

PURCHASING AND SUPPLY 030–039
#032—*Product Testing*   PGP—1

Products to be tested will be identified and distributed to test sites. Following testing the participants will complete a comprehensive evaluation and make recommendations.
Classification: Other Approved Activity
Instructor: To Be Announced
Eligible Participants: All Staff
Location: To Be Announced
Time: To Be Announced
Dates: To Be Announced

ORGANIZING AND PLANNING 400–420
(ELEMENTARY CURRICULUM AND INSTRUCTION)
#400—*Elementary Classroom Demonstrations K-6*   PGP—TBA

Participants will have an opportunity to observe a demonstration teacher using effective classroom planning, management and teaching strategies for success in working with students.
Classification: Content/Methods
Instructor: Elementary Supervisors
Eligible Participants:
Location: To Be Announced
Time: To Be Announced
Dates: To Be Announced

COMPUTER TRAINING 100–145
#116—*Computer Software Review*   PGP—

New and existing software will be demonstrated. Teachers will run the programs. The last ten minutes we will discuss applications of the software in the classroom.
Classification: Curriculum
Instructor: To Be Announced
Eligible Participants: Open
Location: To Be Announced
Time: To Be Announced
Dates: To Be Announced

MULTICULTURE 316–317
#316—*Cross Cultural Teaching Methods and Materials*
(Native American Model) PGP—1

> Participants will gain information/knowledge on teaching children more effectively about Native Americans. Strategies on teaching Indian children and substantial information on resource materials are included.
>
> Classification: Content/Methods
> Instructor: To Be Announced
> Eligible Participants: Open
> Location: To Be Announced
> Time: To Be Announced
> Dates: To Be Announced

FOREIGN LANGUAGE 218–223
#218—*Progress and Planning—French* PGP—1

> A volunteer teacher will make a presentation on an aspect of teaching the language after which participants will discuss and ask questions. When extensive district planning is necessary, this will supplant the foregoing activity.
>
> Classification: Content/Methods
> Instructor: Supervisor et al.
> Eligible Participants: French Teachers
> Location: Junior High School
> Time: To Be Announced
> Dates: To Be Announced

PROFESSIONAL GROWTH
CLASSIFICATION OF ACTIVITIES
7 TRAINING HOURS = 1 POINT

   I. Content and Method (12 points required for each six-year period)
   A. Formal Coursework
   B. Curriculum
  II. Student Assistance (8 points maximum)
 III. Professional Involvement (5 points maximum)
 IV. Supplementary Teaching Responsibilities (5 points maximum)
  V. Other Approved Activities (5 points maximum)
 VI. Community Services (5 points maximum)

MODEL XIV
STAFF DEVELOPMENT EVALUATION

Course Title _____ Course No. _____
Instructor _____ Date _____

The information on this sheet will be reviewed by the Staff Development Office and the course instructor. Candid, constructive suggestions will assist with the effort to improve the quality of the Staff Development Program. Your cooperation is appreciated.

Please answer each question by marking the appropriate item.

		YES	NO
1.	The objectives, as stated, were completed.	____	____
2.	The course provided useful information and ideas.	____	____
3.	The sessions were well organized and comprehensive.	____	____
4.	The instructor provided opportunity for participant interaction.	____	____
5.	The course content/activities will help me improve my performance.	____	____
6.	I would recommend this course to my colleagues.	____	____

Please give specific and concise answers to the following questions.

7. The most valuable thing(s) learned from this activity: _____

8. I am planning to use this course information in the following manner:

9. Additional assistance needed to implement the ideas in this course would_____

Please add comments/suggestions to facilitate effective Staff Development activities. Use other side for additional comments.

_____
_____

GRANTS: VIA MANAGEMENT/ COLLABORATIVE EFFORTS AND STAFF

Grants are numerous and available for the staff developer to provide training in many areas. Most school districts have policies that regulate the requests, the program plans, and the payment procedures. Below are samples of these procedures.

MODEL XV
REQUEST TO APPLY FOR GRANT

Education for Economic Security Act — EESA — Title II
Math and Science Grant

Federal Math/Science Training Support Grant

The finalization of participation in the Education for Economic Security Act funding under Title II has been approved by the State Department of Education. The school district will receive $76,629 for reimbursable staff development activities conducted from April through January 1.

Purpose

Staff development programs planned for the grant will focus on enhancing the teaching methods and content knowledge of teachers in the fields of math and science. The monies will provide for inservice training and retraining of elementary and secondary teachers and other appropriate personnel, including vocational education teachers who use mathematics and science in the course of study. Approved items for staff development are:

> Teacher stipends
> Travel expenses
> Substitute teachers
> Consultant fees
> Materials
> Equipment

Participants

Seven nonpublic schools have chosen to participate with public schools. They have been actively involved in both math and science programs.

Representation from the participating schools will review the original assessment results and current needs to determine training focus.

Budget

MODEL XVI
GRANT ACTIVITIES REPORT

Education for Economic Security Act — Title II
Math and Science Grant

Federal Staff Development Grant

The application to participate in the program of Education for Economic Security Act under Title II has been approved. With School Board approval, the School District will receive $40,399.00 for reimbursable staff development activities conducted through December 31.

Purpose

Staff development programs planned for the grant will focus on enhancing the teaching methods and content knowledge of teachers in the fields of math and science. The monies will provide for inservice training and retraining of elementary and secondary teachers and other appropriate personnel, including vocational education teachers who use mathematics and science in the course of study.

Program

Representatives from the participating schools have defined problem areas and established a focus for which to provide activities for the unmet needs indicated in the survey. They are as follows:

I. Using Manipulative Objects and Concrete Activities to Enhance Achievement of Learning Outcomes K–12

- Series of workshops using manipulative activities K–6
- Problem solving
- Computer Application

II. Exploring the Future of Science Education K–9

- Study Committee K–8
- Articulation Elementary/Junior High
- Demonstration Teaching on Specific Outcomes
- Exposition/Adopt-A-School

III. Mastering Learning Outcomes in Mathematics

- Simple Mathematics
- Geometry
- Problem Solving
- Extensions and Corrections
- Computer Applications
- Study Committee to provide method of horizontal usage within identified outcomes

PROPOSED ESTIMATED BUDGET

• Stipends for teachers to attend in-service programs outside the regular school day	$23,000
• Fees for consultants providing in-service training	5,000
• Travel and related expenses of teachers attending inservice training or consultants providing inservice	6,000
• Materials and supplies necessary for inservice	2,000
• Substitute teachers (public schools only)	4,000
• Other—miscellaneous workshop accommodations	399
	$40,399

Prepared by:

Assistant Superintendent
Staff Development Services

Approved by:

Superintendent of Schools

MODEL XVII
DEVELOPING AGENDAS

MONDAY—June 22nd

12:30–12:45   Introduction and Start Up   Staff Development

CELEBRATING SUCCESS:

12:45–1:15   Discussion of Project Success   Curriculum Director
                       Purpose and Accomplishments   and Participants

- What were the most important goals
- and key concepts of Project Success?
- What personal successes have you experienced?
- What changes have you seen in students?

1:15–1:30	Group Reports	
1:30–1:45	B R E A K	
1:45–2:15	Success from the District Perspective	Research Office Staff Assistant

DETERMINING NEEDS:

| 2:15–2:45 | Group Activity Where do we need to go from teaching viewpoint?
• concerns
• needs
• interests | Participants |
| 2:45–3:00 | Research Division— Analysis of Needs | Staff Assistant |

RECOMMENDATIONS:

| 3:00–3:20 | Where do we need to go from District viewpoint? | Curriculum Director and Participants |
| 3:20–3:30 | Reflections | Staff Development |

TUESDAY—June 23rd

| 12:30–12:45 | Review | Staff Development |
| 12:45–1:15 | A Look at Expected Learning Outcomes | Curriculum Office |

ACTION PLANNING:

1:15–2:30	Creating a new ACTION PLAN	Staff Development
2:30–2:45	B R E A K	
2:45–3:30	Listing of Outcomes and Scheduling Topics for Meetings During the School Year	Curriculum Director

REPORTING TO THE SCHOOL BOARD/ VIA STAFF INVOLVED IN PROGRAM

The staff development activities are noteworthy and regularly reported to the governing board of the district. These should be informative, concise, relevant, and pertain to the stated goals of the Board of Education.

MODEL XVIII
STAFF DEVELOPMENT ANNUAL REPORT
TO BOARD OF EDUCATION

Goals

The specific goals of the staff development program are to:

1. Determine staff development needs of the employees of the school district.
2. Provide staff development courses and activities for certified and classified personnel.
3. Coordinate formulation and implementation of staff development programs at the departmental and building levels.
4. Survey and catalog staff development opportunities available through other organizations and institutions.
5. Facilitate participation in staff development programs of other departments/divisions.
6. Promote staff development participation.
7. Expand staff development relationships with postsecondary institutions.
8. Implement an evaluation and improvement procedure for staff development programs.
9. Identify funding resources for implementing and/or improving staff development programs.
10. Initiate a follow up process to determine the effectiveness of programs.

The major goal of Staff Development Services is to assist staff to grow professionally and personally by focusing on meeting instructional challenges and exploring learning experiences for students. It is a "people" activity with joint decision making responsibilities. Effective programs are those requested by staff who have become a part of the planning, implementing, and evaluating.

Staff members submit proposals requesting specific course offerings. Departments, divisions, supervisors and others become involved in the process. Activities are voluntary and generally scheduled outside the school day, with priorities determined by district-wide goals, needs assessment surveys, and others. Building coordinators are selected to serve as a liaison for the Staff Development Office and assist with communication, registration, program proposals, and facilitation.

Staff members register for activities and receive professional growth points by successfully completing sessions which meet the criteria stipulated in the professional growth guidelines. The majority of the courses are directed by staff, outside consultants, and resource personnel.

STATISTICAL COMPARISON OF
STAFF DEVELOPMENT PROGRAMS

	Year I	Year II	Year III	Year IV	Year V
Number of activities	174	176	246	320	335
Activities cancelled	59	29	24	40	23
Number of staff participating	3,295	4,075	4,442	4,637	9,285
Estimated hours of participation	20,184	20,270	26,516	32,459	72,314

The five-year comparison chart shows the staff involvement and commitment to self-improvement. A sharp increase is noted in number of staff participating. This is due to the increased number of district-wide programs provided for staff through various workshops and training sessions offered this past year. The demand and interest for this type of service accounts for the large number of hours. Many of the work sessions have exceeded the maximum. Summer workshops, administrator training and the need for specific skills have expanded the staff development arena.

Special thanks is extended to Building Coordinators, and to the members of the Staff Development and Professional Growth committees for their cooperation in creating this innovative and comprehensive plan.

Submitted by: Approved by:
Staff Development Services   Superintendent of Schools

MODEL XIX
AGENDA
NEW LEADERSHIP STAFF WORKSHOP

GENERAL ADMINISTRATIVE SERVICES

8:00–8:10 a.m.   Welcome and Introduction Assistant Superintendent
                                             Staff Development Services

8:10–8:25 a.m.	Overview/Office of the Superintendent	Assistant Superintendent
8:25–8:55 a.m.	Administration and Instructional Research	Coordinator Staff Assistant
8:55–9:15 a.m.	Financial Planning	Staff Assistant
9:15–9:30 a.m.	BREAK	
9:30–9:55 a.m.	Communication is a Responsibility	Director
9:55–10:25 a.m.	Educational Data Processing Center	Staff (5)
10:25–11:00 a.m.	State and Federal Relations	Lobbyist
11:00–11:30 a.m.	Questions and Answers	Assistant Superintendent

Objectives

1. To develop an awareness of the functions within General Administrative Services.
2. To become acquainted with key contact staff who perform the functions of General Administrative Services.
3. To understand the management's role in delivering services.
4. To gain an appreciation of the services available to assist building leaders.

MODEL XX
STAFF DEVELOPMENT NEEDS
ASSESSMENT SURVEY RESULTS
TWENTY (20) HIGHEST RANKED ITEMS
AND COURSE OFFERINGS

Staff Development Surveys were completed by 1,601 teachers and administrators. The top-ranked staff development proposed topics for inservice are shown below. Many building and district offerings will be designed to address the topics in which the most interest is shown.

No. of Offerings Provided		*Top Ranked Topics*	*Rank*	*Percent*
(10)	21.	Motivating students and developing responsibility (Student Development)	1	59.8

No. of Offerings Provided		Top Ranked Topics	Rank	Percent
(10)	22.	Promoting positive self-image (Student Development)	2	38.7
(15)	38.	Coping with stress (Knowledge/Information)	3	35.4
(29)	26.	Acquiring computer literacy (Knowledge/Information)	4	34.3
(10)	45.	Promoting effective parent, teacher, student and communication (Communication)	5	33.1
(20)	27.	Applying computer management and word processing (Knowledge/Information)	6	28.6
(12)	10.	Utilizing critical thinking/reasoning skills (Curriculum/Instruction)	7	28.4
(20)	2.	Managing the classroom (Organization and Skills)	8	27.7
(15)	47.	Maintaining administration and staff communications (Communications)	9	26.7
(7)	43.	Improving health through physical fitness (Knowledge/Information)	10	25.5
(26)	3.	Organizing the classroom for learning and instruction (Organization and Planning Skills)	11	25.2
(7)	48.	Developing skills in effective parenting (Communications)	12	25.0
(75)	11.	Developing innovative strategies and methods (Curriculum/Instruction)	13	24.7
(12)	40.	Learning first aid (CPR Workshops) (Knowledge/Information)	14	24.7
(6)	24.	Counseling student (Student Development)	15	24.2
(13)	13.	Teaching computer literacy to students (Curriculum/Instruction)	16	24.2
(83)	4.	Planning and organizing instruction units (Identify subject area: _____) (Organization and Planning Skills)	17	22.9
(8)	18.	Identify learning styles (Curriculum/Instruction)	18	21.7
(11)	6.	Mainstreaming students (Organization and Planning Skills)	18	21.7
(1)	39.	Planning financial security and retirement (Knowledge/Information)	20	19.5

STAFF DEVELOPMENT BUILDING
COORDINATORS' SURVEY SUMMARY
STAFF DEVELOPMENT FOCUS

Number Course Offering	DISTRICT-WIDE PROGRAMS	Needed	Not Necessary
(18)	• Effective Schools, which includes		
	Mastery	48	5
	Motivation	47	4
	Coaching	43	9
	Cooperative Learning	39	7
(8)	• TESA (Teacher Expectations Student Achievement)	46	15

CURRICULUM CONTENT/INSTRUCTION

(23)	• Current Trends	55	5
(56)	• Computer Skills/Technology	54	3
(13)	• Instructional Process	53	7
(10)	• Thinking Skills	53	5
(7)	• Study Skills	47	8
(20)	• Exemplary Teaching Practices	47	5
(12)	• Multicultural/Non-Sexist	30	21

CLASSROOM MANAGEMENT

(15)	• Positive/Assertive Discipline	58	3
(31)	• Instructional Management and Planning	45	10

HUMAN-COMMUNITY RELATIONS

(15)	• Professionalism	47	9
(11)	• Familyness	46	6
(13)	• Staff Morale (Self-Esteem)	40	3
(3)	• SAT (Student Assistance Teams)	36	1

Implementation Model XXI

STAFF DEVELOPMENT TRAINING TO IMPLEMENT MULTICULTURAL/MULTIETHNIC CURRICULUM

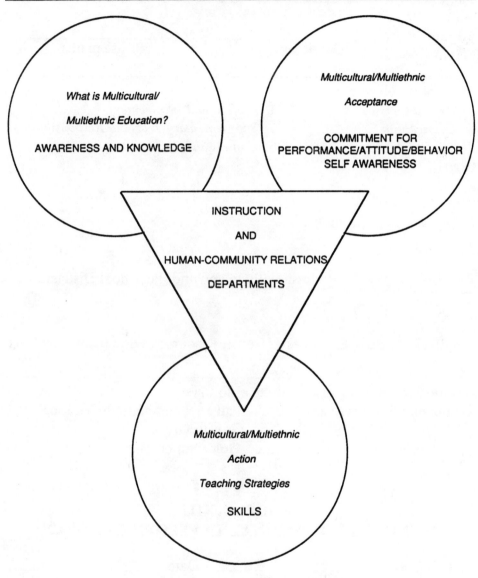

What is Multicultural/

Multiethnic Education?

AWARENESS AND KNOWLEDGE

Multicultural/Multiethnic

Acceptance

COMMITMENT FOR
PERFORMANCE/ATTITUDE/BEHAVIOR
SELF AWARENESS

INSTRUCTION

AND

HUMAN-COMMUNITY RELATIONS

DEPARTMENTS

Multicultural/Multiethnic

Action

Teaching Strategies

SKILLS

MODEL XXII
SIX-YEAR PROFESSIONAL DEVELOPMENT PLAN

Staff Person _____ Date _____
(Please print)

Administrator _____ School _____
(Reviewed by)   (Please print)

_____

Areas of Involvement:

1. *Formal Coursework:*   4. *Professional Involvement:*
2. *Curriculum:*   5. *Supplementary Teaching Responsibilities:*
3. *Student Assistance:*   6. *Community Services:*

Goals
1.
2.

Objectives: (Measurable)
1.
2.

Benefits: Personally/Professionally to you and the School District
1.
2.

Needed Resources: Examples—Human Resources, Equipment, Time, etc.

CC: Supervisor/District Office _____
Optional: Staff member distribute as follows:
White: Staff Member Copy   Pink: Staff Development/Professional
                                 Growth Office
Canary: To/From _____ Gold: Supervisor
(Admin.)

MODEL XXIII
ANNUAL PROFESSIONAL DEVELOPMENT PLAN

Staff Person _____ Date _____
(Please print)

Administrator _____ School _____
(Reviewed by)   (Please print)

_____

Completed Professional Growth Points _____

Professional Growth Period _____ to _____

Developmental Year (please circle) 1 2 3 4 5 6

  I. Six Year Development Goal(s) to be addressed during the current year.

      1.

      2.

      3.

  II. Activity Involvement Supporting the above listed goal(s).

                                         Calendar date of activity.

      1.

      2.

      3.

 III. Anticipated Costs for above listed activities.

 IV. Source of Revenue for anticipated costs.

  V. Professional and Personal Benefits:

CC: Supervisor/District Office _____

Optional: Staff member distribute as follows:

White: Staff Member Copy Pink: Staff Development/Professional
                                 Growth Office

Canary: To/From   _____ Gold: Supervisor
                    (Admin.)

BIBLIOGRAPHY

Baptiste, M., & Baptiste, H. P. (1980). Staff Development for a Large School District. In W. R. Houston & R. Pankratz (Eds.), *Staff Development and Educational Change.* Reston, VA: Association of Teacher Educators.

Bell, C., & Putnam, T. (1979). Mastering the Art of Training Design. *Training and Development Journal, 33,* 24–27.

Caldwell, S. D. (1985). The Master Teacher as Staff Developer. *The Elementary School Journal, 86,* 55–59.

Cornett, C. E. (1986). *Learning Through Laughter: Humor in the Classroom.* Bloomington, IN: Phi Delta Kappa.

Dillon-Peterson, B. (1981). Staff Development/Organization Development— Perspective 1981. *Staff Development/Organization Development.* Alexandria, VA: Association for Supervision and Curriculum Development.

Duncan, M. E., & McCombs, C. (1982). Adult Life Phases: Blueprint for Staff Development Planning. *Community College Review, 10,* 26–35.

Dunne, T. O., & Maurer, R. (1982). Improving Your School Through Quality Circles. *NASSP Bulletin, 66*(457), 87–90.

Edwards, S. A., & Barnes, S. (1985). A Research-Based Staff Development Model That Works. *Educational Leadership, 42,* 54–56.

Eisner, E. (Ed.) (1985). *Learning and Teaching the Ways of Knowledge.* Eighty-fourth Yearbook of the National Society for the Study of Education, Part II. Chicago: University of Chicago Press.

Finn, C. E., Jr. (1987, September). How to Spot an Effective Principal. *Principal, 67,* 20–22.

Flinn, J. Z. (1982). Curriculum Change Through Staff Development. *Educational Leadership, 40,* 51–52.

Fonzi, M. A. (1982). A Critique of "Guidelines for Better Staff Development." *Educational Leadership, 40,* 32–33.

Gall, M. D., & Renchler, R. S. (1985). *Effective Staff Development for Teachers: A Research-Based Model.* Eugene, OR: ERIC Clearinghouse on Educational Management.

Greenfield, W., & Blase, J. J. (1981, November). Motivating Teachers: Understanding the Factors that Shape Performance. *NASSP Bulletin, 65*(448), 1–10.

Harris, B. M. (1980). *Improving Staff Performance Through In-Service Education.* Boston: Allyn & Bacon.

Hibner, D. (1983). Staff Development from the Principal's Perspective. In R. A.

Edelfelt (Ed.), *Staff Development for School Improvement: An Illustration.* Ypsilanti, MI: National Center on Teaching and Learning.

Holly, F. (1982). Teachers Views on In-service Training. *Phi Delta Kappan, 63,* 417–418.

Hughes, C. S. (1981, October). Staff Development for Building Student Thinking Skills. *Educational Leadership, 39*(1), 48–51.

Ihle, R. (1987, September). Defining the Big Principal—What Schools and Teachers Want in Their Leaders. *NASSP Bulletin, 71*(500), 94–98.

Joyce, B., & Showers, B. (1980). Improving In-service Training: The Messages of Research. *Educational Leadership, 37,* 379–385.

Joyce, B., & Showers, B. (1983). *Power in Staff Development Through Research and Training.* Washington, DC: Association for Supervision and Curriculum Development.

Joyce, B., & Showers, B. (1982). The Coaching of Teaching. *Educational Leadership, 40,* 4–10.

Joyce, B., & Weil, M. (1980). *Models of Teaching* (2nd ed.). Englewood Cliffs, NJ: Prentice Hall.

Korinek, L., Schmid, R., & McAdams, M. (1985). In-service Types and Best Practices. *Journal of Research and Development in Education, 18,* 33–38.

Krajewski, R. J. (1981, Fall). Clinical Supervision in the Secondary School: Foundations for Principals. *American Secondary Education, 11*(3), 2–5.

Major, D. (1980). Assumptions About Adult Learning and Staff Development Practices. *The Journal of Staff Development, 1,* 113–118.

McCarthy, B. (1985, April). What 4mat Training Teaches Us About Staff Development. *Educational Leadership,* 61–68.

McCleary, L. E. (1983, November). The Urban Principal: A New Basis for Leadership. *NASSP Bulletin, 67*(466), 8–11.

McRel. (1983). *Coaching: A Powerful Strategy for Improving Staff Development and In-service Education.* Kansas City, MO: The Mid-Continent Regional Educational Laboratory, 40–46.

Orlich, D. C. (1983). Some Considerations for Effective In-service Education. *The Clearinghouse, 56,* 197–202.

Ouchi, W. G. (1981). *Theory Z: How American Business Can Meet the Japanese Challenge.* New York: Avon.

Purcell, L. O. (1987). *Principal's Role in Staff Development.*

Rogus, J. F. (1983, January). How Principals Can Strengthen School Performance. *NASSP Bulletin, 67*(459), 1–7.

Sacks, S. R. (1984, Fall). The Classroom Lives of Teachers: Issues, Observations, and Recommendations. *MEDARP Seminar Series.*

Sadler, W. A. Jr., & Whimbey, A. (1980, Fall). Teaching Cognitive Skills. *National Forum, 60*(4), 40–43.

Sergiovanni, T. J. (1982, February). Ten Principles of Quality Leadership. *Educational Leadership, 39*(5), 330–336.

Showers, B. (1985). Teachers Coaching Teachers. *Educational Leadership, 42,* 43–48.

Stachowski, E. A. (Speaker). (1982). Staff Development. (Cassette recording). New Orleans, LA: American Association of School Administrators.

Sweeney, J. (1982, Winter). Principals Can Provide Instructional Leadership—It Takes Commitment. *Education, 103*(2), 204–207.

The Urban Initiative Sourcebook: A Discussion of the Literature and a Directory of Exemplary Practices and Programs. (1985). Prepared for the Urban Schools of New Jersey.

Thompson, S. R., & Wood, F. H. (1982). Staff Development Guidelines Reaffirmed: A Response to Fonzi. *Educational Leadership, 40,* 34–35.

Wallace, D. G. (Ed.). (1982). *Developing Basic Skills Programs in Secondary Schools.* ASCD.

Wood, F. H. (1982). The Training of Staff Development Facilitators for the School Improvement Project. *The Journal of Staff Development, 3,* 54–65.

Wood, F. H., McQuarrie, F. O., & Thompson, S. R. (1982, October). Practitioners and Professors Agree on Effective Staff Development Practices. *Educational Leadership,* 28–31.

INDEX

117